The
Long
March

Red China Under Chairman Mao

by Don Lawson

The
Long March

Red China Under Chairman Mao

by Don Lawson

illustrated with photographs

THOMAS Y. CROWELL   NEW YORK

Library of Congress Cataloging in Publication Data
Lawson, Don.
  The Long March.

  Includes index.
  Summary: An account of the Communist victory in
China, the rise to power of Mao Tsetung, and the Long
March undertaken by the Red Army in 1934.
  1. China—History—Long March, 1934-1935—Juvenile
literature. 2. Communism—China—History—Juvenile
literature. 3. Mao, Tse tung, 1893-1976—Juvenile
literature. [1. China—History—Long March, 1934-1935.
2. Mao, Tse tung, 1893-1976. 3. Communism—China—
History] I. Title.
DS777.5134.L38 1983   951.04′2   82-45580
ISBN 0-690-04271-X
ISBN 0-690-04272-8 (lib. bdg.)

10 9 8 7 6 5 4 3 2 1

First Edition

To Ruth Yates

World traveler
and old China
hand

Contents

Photograph inserts will be found following pages 90 and 154.

A Note on Language and Pronunciation

There is no wholly satisfactory way to romanize or render the Chinese language into written English. For many years the accepted way to do so was the Wade-Giles system. More recently the government of the People's Republic of China has developed a new system of romanization, called Pinyin. Pinyin has gradually gained acceptance as the international method for rendering Chinese into written English.

In Pinyin words are pronounced phonetically, or made to sound in English as they do in Chinese, roughly as they are written. There are, however, several important exceptions. These are the letters C, Q, and X. C in Pinyin is given a "ts" sound as in "its." Cao is thus read "tsao," with the "ao" sounding like "ow" in "allow." Q is given a "ch" sound as in "cheek." Thus the last or given name of Mao's widow,

Jiang Qing, is pronounced "Ching." (Chinese surnames are written first and given names last.) X in Pinyin is pronounced—with difficulty by English-speaking people—as "hs" with a slight hiss. (In the old Wade-Giles system it was actually written "hs".)

The Pinyin pronunciations of several other important letters are: a as in "far," ch as in "cheap," e is usually given an "uh" sound as in "grunt," g is always hard as in "go," o as in "paw," ou as in "dough," u as in "too," and zh as in "joe."

Although the Pinyin system of romanization has become generally accepted, the Wade-Giles system is still often used for such widely recognized names as Chiang Kai-shek, Sun Yat-sen, China, Shanghai, and the Yangtze River. Widely known names that are often used in either the Wade-Giles or Pinyin system include Mao Tsetung (Mao Zedong in Pinyin), Chou En-lai (Zhou Enlai), Peking (Beijing), Nanking (Nanjing), and Canton (Guangzhou).

By way of example, listed below are some of the names used in this book, showing both the Wade-Giles and Pinyin spellings with the phonetic pronunciation at the right.

Old (Wade-Giles)	New (Pinyin)	Pronunciation
Mao Tsetung	Mao Zedong	Mow dzuh-dawng
Chou En-lai	Zhou Enlai	Joe en-lye
Chu Teh	Zhu De	Jew duh
Sun Yat-sen	Sun Zhongshan	Soon jawng-shan
Hua Kuofeng	Hua Guofeng	Hwa gwaw-fung
Teng Hsiaoping	Deng Xiaoping	Dung hsee-ow-ping
Hu Yaobang	Hu Yaobang	Hoo yow-bahng
Yang Kai-hui	Yang Kaihui	Yahng kye-hway
Chiang Ching	Jiang Qing	Jee-ahng ching

Lin Piao	Lin Biao	Lin bee-ow
Liu Pocheng	Liu Bocheng	Lyew bo-chung
Confucius	Kongfuzi	Kawhng-foodzih

On the map on page 4, most place names and names of physical features are given in Pinyin with the Wade-Giles spelling in parentheses.

—D.L.

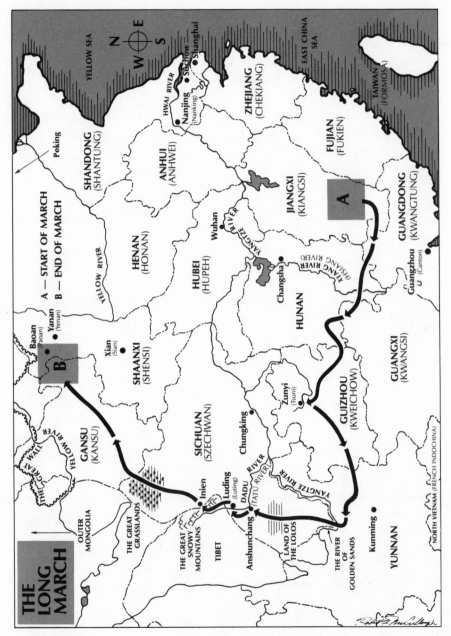

Map by Robert McCullough

1

The Trial of the Gang of Four

Late in 1980 a notorious sixty-six-year-old Chinese woman went on trial for her life in Peking, China. She was Jiang Qing, widow of Communist Party Chairman Mao Tsetung, one of the most famous and important men in modern Chinese history. Until his death in 1976, Chairman Mao had long been China's revered revolutionary leader. Many Chinese, in fact, could remember no leader other than Mao.

Jiang Qing, or Madame Mao, was accused of treason and of persecuting millions of Chinese—at least 35,000 of them fatally. Also on trial with Mao's widow were three men accused of crimes similar to hers. They were the former mayor of Shanghai, Zhang Chunqiao, and two other former top government officials, Wang Hongwen and Yao Wenyuan.

Jiang Qing and her three codefendants were known as "The Gang of Four."

The Gang of Four's alleged crimes had been committed during the last years of Mao Tsetung's life. Mao was still the all-powerful chairman of the ruling Chinese Communist Party, but his health had begun to fail and he feared that his dictatorlike control of the country was also slipping. In addition, he feared that many members of the Communist Party and the Chinese people themselves were losing their revolutionary spirit—the spirit that had changed China from feudalism into a modern twentieth-century society.

The Chinese, Mao believed, were becoming too conservative and capitalistic, thinking mainly of selfish material gains.

"We must return to the spirit of the days of the Long March," Mao said. "Today's young Chinese students read of the Long March and think of it as ancient and dead history. It is not. The days of the Long March must live again."

In 1966 Chairman Mao began a radical program to rekindle the revolutionary fires throughout China. Mao called his new program "The Great Cultural Revolution." The idea behind it was that there should be a permanent revolution in China. The country should once again become a primitive revolutionary society. Schools and universities would be closed because they encouraged an "elite" class system. The nation's economic condition should be ignored because concern about the economy led people to seek middle-class security.

"The role of the revolutionary," Mao said, "is one of never-ending class struggle."

One of Mao's specific weapons in the Cultural Revolution was the creation of the so-called Red Guards. These were young students who were urged to join into bands and attack anyone in authority, including their own parents, who opposed the new Cultural Revolution. This led to widespread book burnings and teenage terrorism of school and government officials throughout China as the young Red Guards rebelled against all forms of authority. Their excuse was that they were recapturing the spirit of the youthful heroes of the Long March who had until now been nothing more than remote figures in their school history books. Youngsters who had been with Mao on the Long March had been known as the Little Red Devils.

What the Cultural Revolution led to was almost complete chaos throughout China. Before its excesses were brought under control, great damage had been done to the society that Mao himself had been mainly responsible for creating. Many observers said that all the good Mao had done for China since the days of the Long March was totally undone in the last years of his life. This, to be sure, was not wholly true, but the Cultural Revolution would darken his people's memory of Mao's last days.

Jiang Qing and her Gang of Four lieutenants took full advantage of the chaos created by the Cultural Revolution to try to gain power in their own right. Chairman Mao realized that this jockeying for power was going on, but by then he was too weak from ill health to prevent it. Later, there were some reports that before his death even Mao himself had tried to establish Jiang Qing as his successor as Communist Party Chairman, but these reports were never confirmed.

One of Jiang Qing's ways of advancing her own authority was to purge public officials who had shown open opposition to the Mao regime. This resulted in thousands of deaths. She also urged the Red Guards to force both university professors and other officials of questionable loyalty to engage publicly in self-criticism for their lack of belief in the Cultural Revolution. Then they were forced to march through the streets of cities such as Peking wearing dunce caps. Those who refused to do so were sent into exile. Some committed suicide.

Madame Mao also laid a heavy hand on the arts. Because she had been a movie actress before she became Mao's third wife, Jiang Qing thought she had special knowledge in this field. Contrary to her own belief, however, China scholar Ross Terrill described her as "a woman with no sense of history, no feeling for the age she was living in, no sensitivity to the masses of the people."

One of Jiang Qing's decrees banished the traditional Chinese opera, which had been a unique and ancient contribution to world culture. To replace it, she decreed there should be "model operas." These were propaganda-filled musical dramas featuring Western-world orchestral accompaniment rather than music by the traditional and ancient musical instruments of China. She also declared that all literature and art must serve the people and the Cultural Revolution. As a result, little but Communist propaganda was published.

Before his death Mao and his top aide, Chou En-lai, tried to undo some of the damage done by the Cultural Revolution in general and the Gang of Four in particular. But they did not wholly succeed. The young Red Guards, for example, were ordered out of the cities and sent into rural areas where, working on farms, they could work off their excess energy as well as live up to their primitive ideals. When they rebelled against becoming slave farm laborers, the Red Army was used to put down the young Red Guard rebellions. Many casualties resulted from these confrontations.

Chairman Mao died on September 9, 1976, at the age of eighty-three. Mao's logical successor would have been Chou En-lai, but Chou himself had died just a few months earlier, on January 8, 1976. Next in line was Hua Guofeng, a man scarcely known outside of Communist Party circles but nevertheless Chairman Mao's handpicked heir. Hua had indicated to Mao that he would consult with Jiang Qing on how to run the country after Mao's death. Hua's assurances to Mao about Jiang Qing, however, were obviously only a political maneuver to curry Mao's favor. A month after Mao's death Hua was named Communist Party Chairman, and the next day he had Jiang Qing and her Gang of Four lieutenants arrested and put in jail. There they remained until November of 1980, when they were put on trial.

The Gang of Four's principal accusers were now Chairman Hua and the Communist Party's Vice Chairman, Deng Xiaoping. Deng had been one of those officials forced to march through the streets of Peking in a dunce cap. Asked before the trial about Jiang's guilt, Deng replied, "She is so evil that any evil thing you can say against her isn't evil enough."

Front pages of the official Chinese press called her "China's devil woman," a "snake," a "scorpion," and "evil incarnate."

The trial of the Gang of Four was a "show" trial. It was held to prove to the Chinese public the Gang's major responsibility for the disastrous Cultural Revolution and thus to solidify the authority of the new government. Guilty verdicts were virtually a foregone conclusion.

Two of the accused dutifully played their roles in the show trial. They were Wang Hongwen and Yao Wenyuan, who said that during the four years they had spent in jail they had seen the error of their ways. Because they admitted their guilt and threw themselves on the mercy of the court, Wang and Yao were not given death sentences. They were, however, given long prison terms.

The former mayor of Shanghai, Zhang Chunqiao—said to be the brains behind the Gang of Four, even more so than Jiang Qing—simply remained defiantly silent from the moment he was brought into court until the trial ended. He was given a suspended death sentence. This uniquely Chinese verdict actually means that the person receiving a suspended death sentence will probably never be executed.

Jiang Qing was openly and loudly defiant from the beginning to the end of the trial. She reaffirmed her firebrand political views and scoffed at the charges of "plotting to usurp the power of the state and to defame leaders of the party and state and of persecuting millions of Chinese during the Cultural Revolution of 1966 to 1976."

Whatever actions she had taken during the Cultural Revolution, Jiang Qing insisted, had been taken at the direct orders of Chairman Mao and of the Communist Party's Central Committee. She did not point out that the Central Committee had then been controlled by the Gang of Four with herself as ringleader.

Jiang completely dominated the six-week trial. Each day she strode regally into court, stood in the defendants' dock, and lashed out at her accusers. Television and news cameras pictured the still handsome, black-haired Madame Mao's open defiance not only for audiences throughout China but also the world. In one of her outbursts, she dared the court to put on an open public debate in Peking's main square. Then, she said, if the public disagreed with her claims she would gladly march to the execution grounds.

When the end of the stormy trial came on January 25, 1981, Madame Mao was sentenced to death. Then, for the last time, Jiang Qing, the former actress and First Lady of China, was dragged from the court, still struggling and still shouting: "Making revolution is right!" and "Long live Chairman Mao!"

But like that of the mayor of Shanghai, Jiang Qing's death sentence was suspended, hers for only two years. During this two-year reprieve she would have an opportunity to repent her actions. At the end of these two years she might be allowed to remain alive but in prison, or, if she still remained defiant, the death sentence could be carried out with a single revolver shot through the back of the head. Few Chinese ever expected to see or hear about Jiang Qing again. She had become what is commonly known, in Communist China as well as in other Communist countries, as a "nonperson."

Early in 1983 China's Supreme Court commuted the death sentences of Jiang Qing and Zhang Chunqiao to life imprisonment. While they had not repented their crimes, it was explained by Chinese officials that they had "not resisted reform in a flagrant way."

Many Chinese thought the verdict on Chairman Mao's widow was too lenient. Some Chinese officials who had suffered torture at her orders during the Cultural Revolution had urged that she be shot. But others, including Party Chairman Hua and Vice Chairman Deng Xiaoping, who had been one of Jiang Qing's chief victims, counseled against execution. Hua, Deng, and the other moderates feared public reaction against the execution of Mao's widow. They also pointed out that there were still living a number of high Party officials who had survived the Long March with Mao and were devoted to his memory. In addition, almost half of the Communist Party's thirty-eight million members had taken part in the Cultural Revolution. Thousands of other new party members had started out as young Red Guards who had burned books and persecuted professors and public officials. All in all, the moderates agreed, it was better to allow Jiang Qing to live— and die—in jail.

But Hua Guofeng, Deng Xiaoping, and the other members of the Communist Central Committee still faced an even more serious problem: what to do about Mao Tsetung. Though dead, Chairman Mao still lived on in the hearts and minds of the great mass of the Chinese people. To many he was like a god. Somehow he must be un-deified, turned back into a real person, a human being with human failings who had made many mistakes during his lifetime.

One of the real if unpublicized reasons for the trial of the Gang of Four was to diminish the historic importance of Mao and to consolidate control of the country in the hands of the new Chinese leaders. But the trial of the Gang of Four had not really dealt with the crucial question of the extent to which Chairman Mao himself was responsible for the Cultural Revolution's decade of turmoil and tragedy.

Somehow, Mao had to be repudiated, cut down to life size, so that the new leaders of China could govern. But at the same time he had to be upheld, because to totally repudiate Mao was to repudiate the foundations of the Chinese Communist Party going back to the days of the Long March and even before. This was the dilemma the present Party leaders now faced.

2

The Attempt to Close Chairman Mao's Little Red Book

When Chairman Mao died, there was a debate among Chinese Communist Party officials about what to do with his body. Should Mao's mortal remains be buried in ordinary fashion, or should his body be permanently preserved and put on public display? Mao himself had said he wanted to be cremated and his ashes "scattered over the rivers and mountains of China" just as had been done with the remains of Chou En-lai.

Chinese Communism had been founded on the political beliefs of two Europeans, Karl Marx and Nikolai Lenin. To the Chinese, Mao was every bit as important as both of these men, and his burial should be at least equal to theirs. But the bodies of Marx and Lenin had each been disposed of in different ways.

Marx was the German author of *Das Kapital* (*Capital*),

the bible of the world Communist movement. Marx died in England in 1883 and was quietly buried in London's Highgate Cemetery.

Lenin was the leader of the Communist movement in Russia and the founder of the Soviet Union. When he died in 1924, his body was preserved or mummified by a special embalming process and put in a tomb in Moscow's Red Square. There it was still on view to thousands of devoted Russians and curious foreign tourists each year. Many Chinese Communists, including Mao himself, had visited Lenin's tomb.

In the end it was the new Chinese Communist Party Chairman, Hua Guofeng, who made the final decision: Mao's body would be mummified and put on display in a mausoleum at the center of Peking in Tiananmen, or the Gate of Heavenly Peace, Square. Hua's usually shrewd political instincts told him that his decision to preserve Mao's body would persuade the Chinese people to identify him with Mao, and this would help Hua keep a firm grip on the country. Already Hua had ordered that his and Mao's pictures be placed side by side throughout the land. Thus, even in death, Mao was called upon to continue to play a key political role in Chinese government.

At Hua's direction embalming specialists were brought in from Vietnam, where they had recently successfully mummified the body of Ho Chi Minh, North Vietnam's Communist dictator. Ho Chi Minh had died in 1969 during the Vietnam War, in which his Vietcong military forces had defeated those of the United States and South Vietnam. Ho's body was now on display in Hanoi, the capital of Vietnam.

The Vietnamese embalmers were successful in preserving

Mao Tsetung's mortal remains. In fact some of China's new leaders soon began to question Hua's decision to keep Mao's body permanently on display. How was it possible to diminish Chairman Mao's godlike image if people throughout China continued to make pilgrimages to Peking to view Mao's body and worship at his shrine? The Mao mausoleum was officially closed from time to time in the vain hope that the Chinese public's interest in Mao's mummy would wane. But then as soon as the mausoleum was reopened to the public, long lines of people gathered once again, waiting patiently to see the body of their lost leader. Soon there was no question but what the new post-Mao Communist Party leaders had a dead body on their hands that they didn't quite know what to do with.

A similar dilemma had faced the leaders of the Soviet Union some years after the death of their dictator, Joseph Stalin. Stalin had been Lenin's trusted aide and succeeded Lenin as the top ruler of the Soviet Union. During World War II Stalin took command of Russia's Red Armies and led them to victory against Adolf Hitler's invading Nazis. After the war Stalin was declared a supreme hero of Russia. Stalin died in 1953, and his specially embalmed body was entombed alongside that of Lenin in Moscow's Red Square. But a few years later the Soviet Union's new dictator, Nikita Khrushchev, began a systematic campaign to destroy Stalin's image as a public hero. Finally, in 1961 Khrushchev's efforts to destroy what he called "the myth that Stalin was Russia's savior" were successful. Stalin's body was removed from the Red Square tomb and reburied among the graves of lesser Red heroes in the walls of the Kremlin, a fortified section of Moscow. His name was removed from the Red Square tomb, public buildings, streets, and factories. Stalingrad, a city that was the site of a great Russian World War II victory and had been named in Stalin's honor, was renamed Volgograd.

No one in China openly proposed such radical steps regarding Mao as had been carried out in the de-Stalinization of the Soviet dictator. But there were certainly those Chinese Communist Party leaders who secretly favored some firm steps in that direction. Among them was Party Vice Chairman Deng Xiaoping, who had gradually begun to emerge as the real power in Chinese government during the post-Mao period. Deng Xiaoping had never been a firm supporter of Hua Guofeng, and less and less was now seen of Hua at important Party functions. A newly prominent leader was Deng's aide, Hu Yaobang, who had recently been named Party Secretary.

China's Communist Party had been founded in 1921. As it approached its sixtieth anniversary in the early summer of 1981, the Party's Central Committee met in secret session to decide both what to do about Mao and the future leadership of China. On July 1, the Party's actual birthday, a dramatic announcement was made to an audience of some ten thousand faithful Communist Party members in Peking's Great Hall of the People: Hua Guofeng was out as Chairman of the Party, and Hu Yaobang was in.

Hua's resignation and Hu's new rise to power were regarded as a great political victory for Deng Xiaoping. Deng had engineered the ouster of Hua, who had been Mao's handpicked successor, and the selection of Hu, who was totally loyal to Deng. More than ever it was clear that Deng Xiaoping was the new strong man of China.

But of even more importance than the selection of a new Party Chairman was a lengthy document that was simultaneously released to the public. This historic communique condemned the "gross mistakes" of the late Mao Tsetung and blamed him for the "catastrophe" of the 1966–76 Cultural Revolution. In launching the decade of violence and turmoil, the document said, "Mao confused the Chinese people with the enemy. The Cultural Revolution conformed neither to Marxism-Leninism nor to Chinese reality."

Both Deng Xiaoping and Deng's new handpicked Party Chairman, Hu Yaobang, as well as the other members of the Central Committee were shrewd enough to realize that outright and total repudiation of Chairman Mao would not be tolerated by all members of the Communist Party or the Chinese public. The once-revered father of modern China could not be suddenly transformed into a monster. Consequently, the historic document released on July 1 acknowledged that, as the Communist Party leadership sought to make China a leading member in the world of nations, they would be guided by Mao's "thought"—his sound revolutionary ideas—but not his "mistaken policies."

Mao's "thought" was dear to the Chinese people. A poet, writer, and philosopher as well as a great political leader, Mao had written hundreds of thousands of words expressing his philosophical and political ideas. Many of the best of these statements had been gathered into a little red book entitled *Quotations from Chairman Mao Tsetung*. Generations of Chinese had grown up using Chairman Mao's Little Red Book as their bible. They obviously were not now about to condemn to outer darkness the author of their bible.

In his inaugural address after becoming Party Chairman, Hu Yaobang scarcely referred to Mao or the document denouncing Mao's failures. Instead Hu told the Chinese to stop looking to the past and encouraged them to train their eyes on the future. In a slight bow to Mao he did say, "We must begin a new 'Long March,' this one based on practical economic policies that will rebuild China's backward economy." Hu also called on the nation's old leaders to begin grooming new, younger leaders who would carry China forward to new greatness in the twenty-first century. "Old Men's Power" was a pet peeve among young Communist Party members.

In encouraging the Chinese people to look to the future and forget about the past, Chairman Hu was encouraging them to forget about Chairman Mao. Thus, like Khrushchev at the beginning of his systematic campaign to destroy Stalin's image in the minds of the Russian people, Hu had now fired the first major salvo in the propaganda barrage to destroy the image of Mao in the minds of the Chinese people. But as far as the late Chairman Mao Tsetung was concerned, the past was not so easily destroyed.

When Joseph Stalin was at the peak of his power in the Soviet Union, his biography filled several pages in the *Great Soviet Encyclopedia*. When Stalin fell from power, owners of the state-sponsored encyclopedia soon received a brief, new, de-Stalinized biography, with instructions to remove the old biography and replace it with this "more truthful" version of Stalin's life story. Many of the few Soviet citizens who were affluent enough to own the encyclopedia dutifully complied, although the move left them with a large blank space in their reference sets.

Citizens of Western democracies find it hard to comprehend such mindless efforts by totalitarian governments to change history simply by rewriting it. But by its very nature the new political party in power in a single-party, totalitarian nation must always be right, and the ousted leaders must always be wrong. This frequently results in what would be a comedy of errors—like tearing out old encyclopedia pages and pasting in new ones—if some of the other results weren't so tragic.

In a democracy, with its multiple political parties, leaders who are defeated in an election simply go about the business of working at some other occupation until the next election. Then they may be voted back into power. Even if they are not, their lives go on much as before. But in a totalitarian state, such as the Soviet Union or China, the new party leaders cannot allow any continuing opposition. To do so would be a sign of weakness. Not only must the old party leaders be proved to have been wrong, but frequently they must also be proved to have committed crimes against the state. Once these frequently trumped-up charges have been "proved," the ousted leaders are all too often put in jail or executed. If a former leader is already dead, his conduct while he was in office must be discredited.

Totalitarian states are called *monolithic.* This means they are like huge blocks of stone on which few changes can be made. Leaders may come and go, but the state remains, unchanged and unchangeable. Since the state is always the same, it is always "right." And because each time new leaders come into power they represent the absolute authority of the state, they too are always "right" no matter what kind of decisions they make. All totalitarian leaders, for example, have always flatly refused to allow freedom of speech, freedom of the press, freedom of assembly, and all of the other freedoms that are taken for granted by the citizens of Western democracies. Such freedoms simply create chaos, dictators say, and make governing a nation impossible. Modern Chinese leaders echo this claim by saying that China, with its low levels of education and technological backwardness, and a population of about one billion people, cannot be granted mass freedom and remain governable without complete chaos. Such freedoms are for the future. But somehow in totalitarian nations that future never seems to come.

As a matter of cold reality, however, not everything in a totalitarian society works out the way its new leaders demand that it work out. Thought control can only be carried so far. Government leaders are dealing with human beings, not robots; not all human beings react the way leaders want them to, no matter how carefully they are programmed.

Not all of the owners of the *Great Soviet Encyclopedia*, for example, destroyed their old Stalin biographies. Many people tore them out of their encyclopedias dutifully enough—just in case an inspector stopped by to see if they had done so—but then they saved them in some safe place to eventually pass on to their children and grandchildren.

And Stalin had never been revered by the Russians as the Chinese revered Mao. Most Russians had feared Stalin as much as they loved him, since they were well aware of the hundreds of thousands of dissidents who had been tortured, slain, or sent to slave labor camps during the Stalin regime. But Stalin *had* once been known as kindly old "Uncle Joe." And he *had* once been a supreme hero of the Soviet Union, who had saved Russia from the Nazi hordes in World War II. That couldn't all have *not* happened. Nor could it be changed overnight. Perhaps a future generation of Russians might like to know some of the facts about Stalin that were more accurate than those given in the new and so-called "more truthful" version of his life.

And so it was in China with the attempted downgrading of Mao Tsetung. There was no official *Great Chinese Encyclopedia* containing his biography that had to be rewritten by the state, but there were dozens of books about him, and these remained as highly prized possessions in many families' meager libraries. Then too there was Chairman Mao's Little Red Book, which was owned by almost everybody. The new Communist Party leaders were going to have virtually an impossible job to close every Little Red Book in China.

Perhaps even more important than books was the word-of-mouth story of Mao's life that was as familiar to most Chinese as a biography of a member of their own family. Much of this oral history of Mao was the stuff of which Chinese legends had been made—legends that would live long into the future, would live in fact long after China's new leaders and the ones who lived after them were dead, buried, and forgotten.

When the Chinese talked about Mao Tsetung, they always talked about two things. These two things were inseparably tied together. They were the Communist revolution, which had shaped modern China, and the Long March, the ordeal by fire that had shaped Mao and his fellow Communist revolutionaries.

3

Boyhood of a Born Rebel

Mao Tsetung always said he had discovered how much could be gained by rebellion when he was still a child. The son of a poor farm family, Mao had to work in the fields each day from dawn until it was time to go to the local primary school. After school he had to return home and again work in the fields until dark. Both his father and his schoolteacher were strict disciplinarians. They frequently punished Mao with physical beatings for real or imagined mistakes.

When Mao was just ten years old, he rebelled against this harsh treatment by running away from home. His plans were vague, but his destination was the city of Changsha, 120 *li* away. (A *li* is about one third of a mile.) Mao never reached the city. He simply wandered around the countryside for several days, lost and hungry. When his family finally found him, Mao was only a few miles from home.

But when he returned home, Mao was somewhat surprised to discover that he was treated much less harshly than in the past by his father—at least temporarily. And back in school, his teacher was also much less severe for the next few months.

"The result of my act of protest impressed me very much," Mao later told journalist Edgar Snow. "It was a successful 'strike.' "

Mao Tsetung was born in a mud hut in the small village of Shaoshan in the province of Hunan in south-central China on December 26, 1893. Interestingly, the people of Hunan have a reputation for rebellious courage. According to one well-known saying, "China can be conquered only when every Hunanese is dead."

In China family names are always stated first and given names last. Thus the future ruler of China's family name was Mao, meaning "Hair," and his given name was Tsetung, meaning "Anoint the East."

Young Mao was the oldest of three brothers, and as such he was supposed to eventually take over the responsibility for the family farm from his father. (There was also a younger sister who, according to Chinese custom, could not become an heir.) But the boy Tsetung had no intention of growing up to become a farmer. He had begun to read widely both in and out of school, and the books he read told him there was a great world outside his village just waiting to be conquered.

In school young Mao was supposed to read the traditional works of Confucius and other Chinese classics. Instead, he and his rebellious classmates got their hands on certain books that had been banned by the school authorities. These were Robin Hood–like tales of adventure and banditry, entitled *Story of the Marshes, The Romance of the Three Kingdoms*, and *Revolt Against the Tang*. In the classroom the boys hid these books behind copies of the classics when the teacher walked past, and thoroughly enjoyed their "study" periods. If they were caught, however, severe punishment immediately followed.

What young Mao objected to most in school was the necessity for blind obedience and the rote recitation of lessons. Students were not allowed to question any statements made by their teacher. They were expected to speak only when spoken to and then, like parrots, they were supposed to respond with memorized stock answers. Often the class was asked to respond in unison, shouting out the rote answers as loudly as possible.

Mao left the village school when he was thirteen. This disappointed his mother, whom the boy loved dearly—perhaps mainly because she always took his side against his father, whom young Mao had begun to hate. The elder Mao was glad to have the boy back on the farm full time; it meant not having to employ a hired hand.

The elder Mao had begun to prosper somewhat not only as a farmer but also as a rice buyer, and when young Mao wasn't doing farm work he was expected to keep the business records. He had learned to use the *abacus*, the ancient Oriental device for adding, subtracting, and multiplying, something his father had never mastered. Young Mao was given no money for his work and very little freedom. He and his father continued to quarrel while the mother tried to be the peacemaker, a role that became increasingly difficult.

Finally, when young Mao was just fourteen, his father decided that what his rebellious son needed was more responsibility. The elder Mao arranged for young Mao to be married to a girl several years his senior. Such arranged marriages were then common in China. Young Mao went through with the wedding ceremony because he was forced to, but afterward he flatly refused to live with his "wife." Mao never considered himself to be married to this unfortunate young woman, and today even her name is unknown.

Young Mao continued to work on the family farm until he was sixteen. Then his mother prevailed upon her husband to let their eldest son leave the village and go to a more advanced school in the city. Her most convincing argument was that an advanced education would enable their son to earn more money. Carrying his luggage on a bamboo pole, young Mao left home without saying good-bye to his father. He never returned there to live.

Mao's eventual goal, as it had been when he ran away from home as a child, was Changsha, the provincial capital. But before going there he stopped off in the nearby town of Xiang Xiang, where his mother's family lived. There Mao lived with his relatives and studied at the East Mountain school until he was almost eighteen. Although he was bigger and older than his classmates and was laughed at as a crude farmer's son, Mao got excellent grades and continued to read widely. But he resented being a social outcast, and in September 1911 he left for Changsha. The only money he had was the equivalent of about ten dollars in Chinese *yuan* that his mother had extracted from his father.

Mao arrived in Changsha, then a city of about 800,000 people, at a time of great political turmoil. Revolution was brewing throughout the land, and the provincial capital was a center of revolutionary activity. Mao was caught up in this activity in a variety of roles for the next several years.

Immediately upon arriving in Changsha, Mao enrolled in an advanced middle school. There he read his first newspapers and became aware of the revolutionary political movement of Dr. Sun Yat-sen. Sun Yat-sen and his followers, including several Hunanese revolutionaries, were trying to bring to an end the tyranny of the Manchu emperors under which the Chinese had long suffered.

Sun Yat-sen opposed the Manchu dynasty that was then ruling China, and was trying to unite the country under a more democratic form of government, such as that of the United States. Called both the "Father of the Revolution" and the "George Washington of China," Sun Yat-sen had been educated at a British medical school in Hong Kong, where he became a physician. But travel outside of China, and especially in America, convinced him that his people were more in need of democracy than doctors. Soon he devoted most of his time to politics.

Sun Yat-sen had sought the financial support of people in the United States, Japan, and Europe to overthrow the Manchus. He got little more than moral support from foreign nations, but he did get strong financial support from the ten million so-called "Overseas Chinese" who lived outside China. He also enlisted the aid of graduates of Chinese military schools in his revolutionary efforts. One of the military school graduates who supported Sun Yat-sen was Chiang Kai-shek, later head of the ruling Kuomintang or Nationalist Party, and eventual enemy of Mao Tsetung.

Mao was destined to spend only a few weeks at the advanced

middle school in Changsha. Shortly after he enrolled, Sun Yat-sen's revolutionary military forces struck in several major Chinese cities. This date, October 10, 1911, afterward became known as Double Ten Day (10/10/11) or Chinese Independence Day, somewhat like the Fourth of July in the United States. It is still celebrated by the Republic of China on Taiwan. Within a few weeks after Double Ten Day, Sun Yat-sen's military forces had captured the major cities in some seventeen provinces in southern China, and the two-and-a-half-century-old Manchu dynasty had fallen.

Along with his classmates, Mao soon became filled with revolutionary fervor. His first revolutionary act was to cut off his pigtail. Long, plaited hair worn in a queue or pigtail was a symbol of loyalty to the traditional Manchu dynasty. One's hair—as well as one's finger- and toenails—was a heritage of one's ancestors and thus should not be destroyed. Some ancient Chinese had prided themselves in their foot-long fingernails, which, of course, made it virtually impossible for them to work. When nails were cut, they were often saved.

Mao's next act of rebellion was to leave school and join Sun Yat-sen's revolutionary army. His army pay was the equivalent of seven dollars a month, most of which Mao spent on revolutionary newspapers and other banned literature.

But by the spring of 1912 the military phase of Sun Yat-sen's revolution had ended. As far as Mao was concerned, the revolution had ended in failure. Although it had succeeded in forcing the Manchu Dynasty to abdicate, it did not succeed in replacing the Manchu government with democracy or a people's form of government. Sun Yat-sen had temporarily been named President of the new Republic, but soon he stepped down and the military came back into power. Mao was convinced that the best form of reform government had not yet been established in China.

Mao resigned from the army and returned to his studies. But he did not immediately return to school. Instead he embarked on a course in self-education by spending every day reading in the city library. Each morning he went to the library as soon as it opened. There he read until noon, when he paused long enough for lunch, which consisted of two rice cakes. Then he returned to the library, where he remained until it closed. His reading ranged far and wide—from economics to natural history to law to history.

By the spring of 1913 Mao had decided to become a teacher. He enrolled in Changsha's Teachers' Training School in 1913, making his way on a scholarship and a small amount of money from home. For the next five years he devoted himself to his teacher training courses, but more and more he found himself becoming interested in politics. This interest grew out of the vast amount of reading he continued to do, much of which centered around the history of his own country. As a young schoolboy he had ignored the study of history mainly because he was bored by the Chinese classics—"I hated Confucius from the time I was eight," Mao once said. But now he realized that in order to take part in the creation of a new China, he would first have to understand the old China.

4

The Old China

The Confucius whom the young Mao and his classmates had come to hate was actually one of the first Chinese scholars to set down the early history of his country. Born about 500 years before Christ, Confucius was a teacher and philosopher who gathered together the sayings and recorded the events in the reigns of two of China's earliest emperors, Yao and Shun. These two emperors lived at least two thousand years before Christ and were among China's most benevolent and beloved rulers.

Confucius himself firmly believed in and taught the values of just and honest government. "Oppressive government," he wrote, "is fiercer and more feared by the people than a tiger." He believed in the popular election of public officials but could get little support for this belief in his time. He also taught,

"What you do not like done to yourself, do not do unto others," long before Christ stated the Golden Rule.

Greatly loved during his life, Confucius became almost a god after his death. His teachings were gathered into the *Five Classics,* which were widely used in Chinese schools, as young Mao had early discovered. They also became the bible of Confucianism, one of China's three most popular religions, along with Buddhism and Taoism. Later there were also many Chinese Christians, but their total number never rivaled the membership in the three Chinese denominations.

One of the things the Chinese never understood about Christianity was its demand that if one were a Christian he could not also belong to another faith. The Chinese saw no harm— in fact felt there might well be future benefits—in belonging to several religious sects. The most universal system of traditional belief in China has always been ancestor worship, which encompasses several religions.

Actually, Confucianism was more a code of ethics than it was a religion, a moral system, somewhat similar to the Christian ethic, under which the nation was supposed to be governed and people tried to live their daily lives. By Mao's time this code had become so frozen and committed to the past that there was widespread feeling that it had lost touch with reality.

Curiously, the lives of Confucius and Mao seemed to have had remarkable parallels. Both were teachers and philosophers. Both believed in a people's government. The Confucian teachings that became a Confucianist bible were not unlike the *Quotations from Chairman Mao* that became a Maoist bible. Finally, there was the near deification of both men after their deaths. One suspects that had the embalming experts been available in China in Confucius' time, his body too might well have been mummified and preserved for public viewing.

Despite Confucius' teachings, the Chinese had no experience of a people's government for centuries after his death. The nation's numerous kingdom states were ruled autocratically by a long series of emperors and warlords.

The first emperor to try and unite these various warring states was Shih Huang-ti, who ruled in the third century before Christ. He headed the Chin dynasty. Shih Huang-ti used slave laborers to build the Great Wall of China by linking together shorter walls built by earlier rulers. The Great Wall was built to keep northern barbarians from invading China. One of the manmade wonders of the world, it still stretches over 1,500 miles across China's rugged and vast plains. It is from fifteen to fifty feet high and from fifteen to twenty-five feet thick.

And the Great Wall did keep the barbarians out of China for many centuries. Following the fall of the Chin dynasty after the death of its emperor, the Han dynasty ruled for 400 years. When it fell in the third century after Christ's birth, China once again became a group of states ruled by separate warlords. In the seventh century A.D. the Tang dynasty was founded and once again succeeded to a degree in uniting the nation. During the Tang dynasty and the Sung dynasty, which immediately followed it, there was a Golden Age in China in which the nation became one of the cultural centers of the world. Poets, artists, musicians, scholars, and scientists flourished. The magnetic compass, gunpowder, and movable type for printing were invented.

But in the thirteenth century this Golden Age was interrupted when Mongol warriors breached the Great Wall and swept down in hordes from the north. Soon China as well as the rest of Asia fell under Mongol rule.

Mongol leader Kublai Khan, the grandson of Genghis Khan, established the Yuan dynasty in China. It was while Kublai Khan ruled that the Venetian trader Marco Polo traveled widely in China—which he called Cathay—and returned home to tell of the riches to be found in the Far East.

In the fourteenth century the Chinese revolted against the Mongols and drove them out of the country. Under the newly established Ming dynasty, Chinese art, literature, and the sciences once again began to flourish. The Ming dynasty lasted for about three hundred years. It in turn was toppled by an invasion from the north in 1644. These invaders were Manchus—from the area known as Manchuria. They established a dynasty that ruled until 1911, when it was overthrown by Dr. Sun Yat-sen's revolutionary armies. The struggling new Republic of China was established in 1912.

Marco Polo was not, of course, the only traveler to spread the word of China's splendors into the West. From the sixteenth century onward traders in increasing numbers from throughout the western world made their way to China by difficult overland and hazardous sea routes. By the nineteenth century, Portuguese, Dutch, French, German, British, and American merchants were trading regularly with China. Always suspicious of "foreign barbarians and devils," however, the Chinese severely restricted these traders' movements within their country. Most traders were restricted to Canton and Macao, which were port cities, and not allowed into the interior.

As events were to prove, the Chinese had legitimate reasons for their distrust of foreigners. One of the chief items used for trading with the Chinese, especially by the British, was the narcotic drug opium. The drug had been in great demand ever since Arab traders had first introduced it into India and

China in the Middle Ages. Early in the nineteenth century the British began to exploit that demand with opium from British-held India. The Manchus' Ching government finally banned the importation, in 1839. That same year the Chinese government seized a shipload of the illegal drug aboard a British ship at Canton and destroyed it. Almost immediately Britain, which not only wanted to maintain its rich opium market but also to open up other profitable trading areas, declared war on the hapless Chinese.

In the so-called "Opium War" that followed, the Chinese were badly defeated. As the price for their defeat they signed the Treaty of Nanking in 1842, which ceded Hong Kong to the British, opened up five additional "treaty ports" to foreign trade, and allowed the opium trade to continue. The British were also paid an indemnity for the opium the Chinese had destroyed.

Immediately other Western nations complained about China's favoritism toward the British and demanded equal trading rights. The United States was instrumental in getting China to end the British trade monopoly, and by the turn of the twentieth century there were some seventy Chinese treaty ports where foreigners could own property and conduct business freely. There was even some talk of dividing up the country among the various most powerful Western nations into "spheres of interest." Again the United States stepped in, this time on China's side, and demanded what was called an "Open Door Policy" for China. Under this policy all of the Western nations were granted free trade in China, but in return had to guarantee China's independence.

Resentment of foreign intrusion in China finally led to the so-called Boxer Rebellion. Many thousands of Chinese belonged to an organization known as the Society of the Righteous Fists, whose aim was to bring to an end all foreign influence in China. One of the curious beliefs of "The Boxers," as Americans and Europeans called them, was that they were immune to bullets. In 1899 the Boxers began to test their immunity by raiding mission stations set up throughout China by foreign Catholic and Protestant churches to convert the Chinese to Christianity.

Many thousands of Chinese had taken enthusiastically to Christianity since its introduction to the country in about the ninth century. One of the most enthusiastic converts to Protestant Christianity was a modern warlord, General Feng Yuhsiang (1882–1948), who was known as "the Christian general." Feng used firehoses to baptize entire regiments in his army. The Boxers, however, regarded all such converts as traitors.

In their terrorist raids the Boxers killed a number of American and European missionaries as well as their Chinese converts. Those missionaries who escaped fled to their various government legations, which were located in a special "forbidden area" in Peking. Some of the resentment of the Chinese may be understood from the signs that appeared in this area as well as in certain Peking parks. They read: "No Dogs or Chinese Allowed." By June of 1900, this foreign legation area was under siege by the Boxers.

At this time the Manchu dynasty that ruled China was headed not by an emperor but by an empress named Tzu Hsi. Tzu Hsi, who was called the Dowager Empress, liked to compare herself with Britain's Queen Victoria. Since, like Queen Victoria, she wanted all of her subjects to love her, the Dowager Empress did not discourage the Boxers in their campaign against the "foreign devils." She also feared that an attempt to suppress the Boxers might make them turn on her government and overthrow the Manchu dynasty. Her decision led to disaster.

Alarmed by the siege situation their citizens were being subjected to in Peking, the United States and several European governments sent troops to capture and occupy Peking. The American effort was led by a battalion of Marines. The Marines headed a rescue force of some 20,000 men from eight foreign nations that fought its way through the streets of Peking and rescued the 17,000 besieged foreign nationals in mid-August 1900. To prevent her capture, the Dowager Empress fled Peking shortly before it fell to the victorious Marines and their allies.

Although the Boxer Rebellion failed in its immediate goals, it was actually the first major step toward modern Chinese nationalism. The Boxer Rebellion had a continuing and growing influence on Chinese public opinion, and it greatly encouraged the revolutionaries led by Sun Yat-sen. As one historian, Dick Wilson, has pointed out, "The Boxer Rebellion was the curtain raiser for the revolution of 1911–12 in which the Nationalists or Kuomintang overthrew the Manchu Dynasty."

Meanwhile, Mao Tsetung, the young revolutionary, was waiting in the wings and about to receive his cue to enter the drama as a principal player.

5

The Making of a Revolutionary

Mao Tsetung graduated with honors from the Teachers' Training School in Changsha in the spring of 1918. But Mao was still trying to find himself—"My right road in life," as he put it. His mother had died during his last year in school, and he still felt lost and lonely. He decided not to take a job as a teacher. Instead he journeyed to Peking and went to work at that city's National University as an assistant librarian, a job he obtained through a former teacher.

It was a lowly position. Mao's salary of just a few dollars a month was barely enough for him to exist on. "My office was so low that people avoided me," Mao said later. He rented sleeping quarters in a small room with seven other young men. "At night," Mao said, "I had to warn people on each side of me when I wanted to turn over."

But Mao was happy in Peking. Always a believer in physical fitness, he now became something of an exercise addict, taking all-day hikes, doing calisthenics, and insisting on daily cold showers. Today he probably would be a jogger and enter running marathons.

Perhaps most important of all, Mao met and fell in love with Yang Kai-hui, daughter of a university professor who had been one of Mao's teachers. For her the young assistant librarian managed to find time to write several of his best poems. He also decided that if he was going to be married, he had to get a better-paying job. In the early spring of 1919 Mao returned to Changsha, where he took a job as a teacher in a primary school.

A few months later, on May 4, a student political uprising began in Peking and soon spread across the country. This uprising, called "The May Fourth Movement," proved to be the real watershed between the Old and the New China. During it Mao Tsetung began to "find his road."

The cause of the youth rebellion was the Versailles Peace Treaty, which had just been signed a year after the end of World War I in Europe.

Although China had not played a major role in the war, it had been an official belligerent on the side of the victorious Allies over Germany and the other Central Powers. At the request of Britain and France, China had also sent some 200,000 coolies, or unskilled laborers, to carry ammunition and supplies behind the battlefront in France. Because of its real if minor role in the conflict, China had a place at the peace table, and many Chinese, especially the nation's idealistic university students, expected great things for China to grow out of the official peace terms. They were disappointed.

At the Versailles Peace Conference in 1919, United States President Woodrow Wilson proposed Fourteen Points for international justice. Wilson also proposed a League of Nations to permanently preserve world peace. Mao, along with many other Chinese young people—young people throughout the world, for that matter—were captivated by the inspirational American president and his vision for the future.

One of Wilson's Fourteen Points was the principle of "self-determination" for all nations. The Chinese assumed that this principle would apply to China and that foreign interference in their country would come to an end. The first test of the self-determination principle ended in abject failure—as Wilson's dream of world peace also ended.

Before World War I Germany had owned a number of concessions, or rights to land in China that was used for docks, railroads, and warehouses. The Chinese assumed that all of this land would now revert to them. But Japan had played a major role in defeating Germany and consequently had a louder voice at the peace table. The Japanese wanted the former German concessions turned over to them. They were especially interested in all areas that would give them access to or control of Manchuria, which they had long coveted. In the end Japan got what it wanted, and China's "rights" were ignored.

Mao, along with thousands of other young Chinese, was angered by this turn of events. But Mao was not exactly surprised. He had followed the course of the war and of the subsequent peace talks, not just by reading newspapers but also by talking with university friends who had recently returned from Europe. These young students had been members of work-study groups who had gone abroad to study world conditions and make plans for the postwar peace in China. Their reports made it clear that China was generally regarded as a third-rate power, and that few foreigners had any respect for the Chinese government.

Typical of the disrespect shown the Chinese abroad was the treatment of the Chinese coolies who had been sent to aid the war effort in France. They had been used as little more than beasts of burden. Treated like animals during the war, afterward they were not only ignored by the major Allies but also abandoned by their own government. Many died of disease in the harsh, alien environment. Few would ever return home.

The May Fourth Movement caused a great stir in China, and for a time it almost restored Sun Yat-sen to power. But it did not succeed in overthrowing the military government, which had steadily increased in strength since Sun Yat-sen had had to step down as the first President of the Republic of China shortly after he took office in 1912. What it did succeed in doing was to introduce Communism into the country. Since Woodrow Wilson and democracy had let China down, many of the disappointed students asked, why not try the form of revolutionary government that had recently been established in Russia?

Russia had fought on the side of the Allies in World War I. But it had dropped out of the fighting in 1917, before the war ended. Then there had been a Russian revolution to overthrow the centuries-old tyranny of the hereditary czars, who were similar to China's emperors. This Russian tyranny was replaced with government by the people, called the Soviet Union, based on the political theories of Karl Marx and Nikolai

Lenin. The Communists believed that all property should be held in common by the people. But first the people had to unite to overthrow the government.

The Marxist-Leninists also had a political organization aimed at spreading their teachings to other countries. It was called the Communist International. The May Fourth movement in China made that country a fertile ground for the growth of Communism. Within a few months the Russian Communists were making overtures to the Chinese student revolutionaries, as well as to Sun Yat-sen, who was still a powerful, much-loved leader. Soon a Society for the Study of Marxism was established at the National University in Peking. Similar societies then began to be established throughout China, including one in Changsha in Hunan Province, in which Mao Tsetung became a charter member.

Mao had read Marx's *Das Kapital* and the *Communist Manifesto*, and they seemed to put into words everything he had been thinking but up to now had been unable to express. When Communism arrived in China, Mao welcomed it with open arms. He became a confirmed Marxist-Leninist almost immediately, and never looked back.

Mao was made the Communist organizer for Hunan Province. He rapidly became the most successful Communist recruiter and organizer in China. He kept his teaching job as a cover-up, but soon he had recruited more than six hundred Marxist converts.

Mao's activities, however, could not be hidden for long from the authorities. Finally he was forced to resign his teaching position and to flee Changsha before he was arrested by the police for revolutionary activity. Mao returned to Peking, where he married Yang Kai-hui in 1920. Actually they were not immediately married but simply began to live together as man and wife and were married later. Mao's wife worked as a youth leader and became one of the most active women Communists.

The Marxist movement also spread rapidly throughout the rest of the country. By July 1921 there were enough Marxists in China to officially establish their own national Communist organization. This occurred in Shanghai, and Mao was on hand to become one of the founders of the China Communist Party (CCP).

The CCP continued to grow rapidly, but advisers sent from Russia pointed out that in order to gain enough strength to overthrow the military government, the Communists should unite with Sun Yat-sen's Nationalist Party. Both the CCP and the Kuomintang were at first reluctant to join forces, but finally they agreed to do so. This agreement was sealed at the first Congress of the Nationalist Party, held in Canton in June 1924.

Again assisted by the Russians, the Kuomintang then established the Whampoa Military Academy at Canton to train revolutionary army officers. The head of this academy was Sun Yat-sen's aide, Chiang Kai-shek.

Born in Chekiang Province in 1887, Chiang came from a family that was far more prosperous than Mao's. Chiang was the son of a middle-class wine merchant, and his family regarded themselves as members of the elite. They encouraged Chiang from an early age to study for an important future role in government. They were disappointed when he decided that the quickest route to authority in China was to follow a military career. He studied at military schools in China and then in Japan at the Military Staff College there.

It was while Chiang was in Japan that he met Sun Yat-sen, who was trying to gain support from the Japanese to overthrow the Manchus. Chiang became a disciple of Sun Yat-sen and in 1911 joined in the revolt that established the Chinese Republic. When Sun Yat-sen was forced to resign after a brief term as president, Chiang went into temporary exile in Japan. When the Communist movement began to gain strength in China, Chiang went to the Soviet Union to study Russian military and political methods. Sun Yat-sen had recalled him from Moscow to take over the top post at the new military academy in Canton, which soon became a stronghold of the Kuomintang forces.

Meanwhile, Mao Tsetung and his wife had returned to Changsha. The order for Mao's arrest had been withdrawn despite the fact that he continued to carry on his Communist activities. In 1921 the Maos' first son was born. He was named Anying. A second son, Anqing, was born the following year.

In 1922 Mao organized and led several industrial strikes, including a coal miners' strike in Hunan Province that resulted in an order for his arrest being reissued by the provincial governor. Mao was forced to separate from his wife—the two years they spent in Changsha made up the longest period they would ever be together—and go into hiding. Nevertheless, Mao continued to recruit CCP members and to stir unrest among industrial workers not only in Hunan Province but also in such major cities as Canton and Shanghai. During the next two years Mao recruited some fifty thousand workers as CCP members and organized more than a dozen strikes.

For his efforts Mao was elected to the powerful Central Committee of the Chinese Communist Party. When Mao received orders from the Central Committee's Russian advisers in 1924 to coordinate his revolutionary activities with the Kuomintang, he was reluctant to do so. He did not believe that the Nationalists really favored a people's government for China as did the Communists. Nevertheless, he tried to carry out his orders. Discipline came hard to Mao, but discipline was a part of Communist doctrine, and Mao was a confirmed Communist.

On March 12, 1925, Sun Yat-sen died. Immediately there began a scramble for control of the Kuomintang. As head of the Whampoa Military Academy, Chiang Kai-shek had not only begun to train hundreds of new officers but had also recruited thousands of new enlisted men to serve under them. Chiang now seized control of all the Nationalist and Communist revolutionary military forces and was thus in effect the new leader of the Kuomintang.

Chiang also soon decided that the time was ripe to seize control of the government of China. The way to do so, he believed, was to capture the nation's key cities in northern and central China. Chiang's timing was sound, and his military forces performed superbly despite their relatively short training. Soon city after city began to fall to the Kuomintang. By 1927 Chiang and his conquering army were at the gates of Shanghai.

The reasons for what happened next at Shanghai have never been quite clear to historians. The event was brutally clear. Chiang suddenly ordered his Kuomintang forces to attack all Communists and Communist sympathizers in the city and to destroy them.

There were many thousands of Communists in Shanghai. It was a large industrial city, and Mao and his comrades had done their recruiting work well. Numerous Communist trade unions had been formed, and industrial workers were threatening to strike and bring the industrial life of the city to a halt. It is believed that Chiang was encouraged by city officials and wealthy businessmen to launch his attack against the Communists so that these trade unions could be destroyed. In any case, then and in the future Chiang received much financial aid not only from local business interests but also foreign business interests who wanted to eliminate trade unions or at least keep them under tight control.

Within a few weeks, thousands of Communists were killed by the Kuomintang in Shanghai and in Canton. A near death-blow had been dealt the Chinese Communist movement. But the blow was not quite fatal.

Mao was not in Shanghai when Chiang's forces attacked. He was in southern China continuing his recruiting work. But he soon had word of what had happened from Communist workers fleeing the massacre and from Communist soldiers who, after refusing to take part in the attack, had also fled south to join Mao. These refugees formed the nucleus of a military force that Mao would use to strike back against Chiang.

Mao had never wholly trusted the Kuomintang, and now Chiang's action had confirmed Mao's suspicions. Mao was not so much disappointed in Chiang as he was with himself. He was sorry he had spent so much time organizing industrial workers in Shanghai and Canton. He had done so mainly because the basic Communist doctrine said that the industrial workers of the world were the ones who should unite and revolt against the factory owners and businessmen who were their oppressors. The *Communist Manifesto* virtually ignored the rural peasants, referring only to "the idiocy of rural life."

But Mao did not regard the peasants as idiots. Far from it. Mao thought the peasants, who made up 85 percent of China's population, should form the backbone of any revolt against Chinese tyranny.

Mao's views about the peasants, not the industrial workers, leading the revolution had gotten him into trouble with Communist Party leaders both in China and in the Soviet Union. Now he regretted that he had not spent all of his time organizing the peasants into a revolutionary army. From this point forward, he resolved, that was exactly what he would do.

6

The Long March Begins

Shortly after Chiang Kai-shek's treacherous 1927 attack on his Communist allies, all the Russian advisers to China's Communist Party left for home. They fled for their own safety. But they continued to send advice to Mao and his fellow members on the Central Committee regarding counterattacks against Chiang. These attacks were to begin immediately against Shanghai and Canton. They were to be made with the largest forces the Chinese Communists could muster, and they were to be direct frontal assaults. Mao thought the advice was foolhardy. He decided to ignore it.

But there were some loyal Chinese Communists who took Moscow's advice. One of these men was a general named Zhu De, who had already organized a small body of troops that he had planned to use as allies of Chiang's Kuomintang forces.

Now he used them against Chiang in what was called the "Autumn Harvest" uprising. The Autumn Harvest uprising was a disastrous failure, and Zhu De and the remnants of his forces fell back to join Mao Tsetung in Hunan, where Mao had already begun to recruit his own peasant army.

Zhu De's and Mao's combined forces then retreated to a rugged mountain area in nearby Jiangxi Province. They numbered about 10,000 men, but their ranks were rapidly swelled by additional refugee soldiers and workers fleeing from Chiang's Kuomintang army. Mao and Zhu De called their military organization the Fourth Red Army. It was destined to become one of the most famous armies in Chinese history. As it continued to expand, however, it was re-formed into the First Army Corps and then into the First Front Army. It was under the latter name that it would march into history.

One of the men who joined the Fourth Red Army in its mountain stronghold was Chou En-lai, who would eventually become Mao's chief aide and lifelong friend. Although Chou came from a well-to-do conservative family, he had been a radical from his youth. But for many years this was an intellectual radicalism, since Chou had very little firsthand knowledge of the life of China's peasants and workers.

Chou was born in 1898 in Chekiang Province, where Chiang Kai-shek had been born a year earlier. Like Chiang, Chou also studied abroad and then served in a top post at the Whampoa Military Academy. To broaden his experience, the Central Committee then sent Chou to Shanghai to organize the industrial workers there into trade unions. Here he had his first eye-opening introduction to the misery and poverty of the average factory worker.

Chou was in Shanghai when the massacre of the Communists

began there but managed to escape. Soon afterward he was made a member of the CCP Central Committee. This made him equal in rank to Mao, and for a time Mao and Chou were rivals for control of the CCP. This rivalry began soon after Mao began to organize the Fourth Red Army area in Jiangxi Province into a civil government patterned after similar local governments in Russia.

The basic unit of this government was called a "soviet." In simple terms, a soviet is defined as a piece of territory administered and governed by representatives of the Communist Party. In greater detail and under ideal circumstances, a soviet is supposed to be a council for each town composed of representatives of the peasants, the workers, and the army. Each local soviet is supposed to decide all matters for the town and send delegates to provincial congresses. These congresses in turn send delegates to national and international congresses.

Ideally again, the people's needs and requests and problems are supposed to flow upward via the various delegates directly to the top Communist Party leaders, and the leaders' responses—in the form of solutions, recommendations, and decisions—are supposed to flow back downward directly to the people. This is called "Democratic Centralism." Actually, of course, no such ideal conditions ever exist since Communists, like everybody else, are human beings subject to error, dishonesty, greed, venality, vanity, selfish ambition, and all of the other frailties that humanity is heir to. The soviet established by Mao and his comrades, though modest in scale, nevertheless aimed at all of these lofty ideals, just as is the case with idealistic political efforts throughout the world.

While Mao and his people were establishing their soviet

in southeast China, a similar though even more modest soviet was being established by Chinese Communists in Shaanxi Province in northwest China. While this northwest soviet was never so large as the one in Jiangxi Province, both soviets became rallying areas for Communists throughout the land. They also became the main targets for Chiang's steadily increasing efforts to destroy the Communist Party in China. He believed that one party and one party only could rule the nation, and that party was the Kuomintang. "The bandits," as Chiang called the Communists—he never referred to them by name—must be annihilated.

During the course of the next several years, Chiang mounted five "annihilation campaigns." In one of these campaigns all of the Communists were driven out of Changsha, and Mao's wife and two sons were captured. Yang Kai-hui was given the opportunity to repudiate Mao and Communism. When she refused to do so, she was executed. This was in 1930. Both of the Maos' sons were rescued by friends and hidden until they could be spirited out of the country and sent to safety in Russia. There his younger son, Anqing, studied to become an engineer. The older son, Anying, also studied in Russia but returned to China in 1948, where he joined the military. When China intervened against South Korea and the United States in the Korean War, Anying was the commander of a division in the Chinese People's Volunteer Corps. He was killed on October 25, 1950.

The Fourth Red Army was much smaller than the Kuomintang army. Mao and Zhu's forces never numbered more than 85,000 poorly equipped men, while Chiang was able to muster as many as 200,000 well-equipped combat troops. For this reason Mao strongly opposed any frontal attacks or head-on confrontations with the Kuomintang. He did not believe in fighting any traditional battles of mass attack and counterattack. In this he continued to be opposed by the Communist Central Committee, including Chou En-lai. For a time Mao was even threatened with permanent expulsion from the CCP.

Nevertheless, Mao insisted that the Fourth Red Army be trained in the guerrilla warfare methods of ambush and retreat. He set down his philosophy of guerrilla warfare in his Little Red Book. It was:

When the enemy advances, we retreat.
When he camps, we harass.
When he tires, we attack.
When he retires, we pursue.
Our weapons are supplied us by the enemy.

Using these guerrilla tactics, the Fourth Red Army was successful in fighting the Kuomintang to a standstill in four of its five annihilation campaigns between 1930 and 1934. (These same tactics were later used with equal success by the Vietcong in the Vietnam War.) Nevertheless, Chiang's determination to wipe out the "Red bandits" never wavered.

In 1931 there was a new turn of events in the struggle for China. Japan invaded Manchuria, the rich industrial northeast corner of China. This was Japan's first step toward gaining control of the whole of East Asia and would eventually lead to the entry of the United States into World War II.

Chiang, however, was so obsessed with his anti-Communist campaign that he ignored the Japanese invasion. In fact he went so far as to order the few Kuomintang forces that were in Manchuria to leave the area, a decision that was extremely unpopular throughout China. While Chiang carried on his futile efforts against the Communists between 1931 and 1934, the Japanese consolidated their gains against the local warlords in Manchuria.

In 1934 Chiang mounted what he called his "final annihilation" campaign. He decided to use virtually all of his best Kuomintang troops to encircle the entire Jiangxi soviet area. Gradually this circle would be drawn tighter and tighter until the Fourth Red Army would have no choice but to give up its guerrilla tactics and stand and fight.

Chiang went about his military encirclement campaign in classic military fashion. He built a series of small forts or blockhouses around the Red Army area and then proceeded to wipe out all enemy resistance between one fort and the next. Once this was done, he built another series of blockhouses in a tighter circle around the enemy and went through the same mopping-up operation yet once again. By the late summer of 1934 the Communist leaders within the Jiangxi soviet realized they must break out of the Kuomintang encirclement or face the annihilation Chiang had long promised them.

Once the decision to break out was reached, there immediately began a debate on how it should be done. Mao insisted that the Red Army should slip through the siege lines in small units and reassemble beyond the Kuomintang blockhouses. The other members of the Central Committee, including Chou En-lai, insisted on a mass breakout. In the end, this latter view prevailed.

Early in October some 85,000 Red Army troops and 15,000 civilians, including thirty-five women and more than one hundred children, began to assemble in the Jiangxi soviet area. The women were mainly the wives of Party officers, including Chou En-lai and Mao Tsetung. Soon after Yang Kai-hui's death Mao had taken another bride. She was a twenty-year-old Party worker named Ho Tzu-chen, whom Mao had lived with since she was a teenager. Ho was now pregnant with their third child but insisted nonetheless on accompanying Mao. In the nine years Ho and Mao would live together she would bear five children.

Many old and infirm people and babes-in-arms were left behind at Jiangxi, including the two Mao infant sons who were too young to walk. They were left with a peasant family, and their parents would never see them again. To accompany the exodus a child had to be in top physical condition and be able to contribute to the common cause. Among the children were a number of eleven- and twelve-year-olds who would act as buglers—somewhat like the drummer boys in the American Civil War—supply carriers, and messengers. All the young people were affectionately known as "The Little Red Devils."

Despite the fact that he opposed the method decided upon for breaking out of their encirclement, once the decision was made Mao threw himself into the preparations for it with a will. Preparations were necessarily few. Food supplies were already low, with the rice ration down to twelve ounces per person per day. Civilians would simply have to carry as much rice and clothing as they could, along with whatever personal possessions they needed. These latter turned out to include spinning wheels, sewing machines, and other cumbersome household articles, all of which proved equally useless in the difficult days ahead. They were loaded onto the backs of donkeys and even water buffaloes. Soldiers, of course, would have to carry their weapons and ammunition as well as rice and water, which was also rationed. Along the way they would somehow have to live off the land. Some of the Party officers were able to round up a few horses and ponies to carry their equipment, including several small printing presses.

Despite the fact that he was recovering from a recent bout of malaria, Mao volunteered to be a member of the advance party that was to lead the way in the breakout. These advance troops left their Jiangxi base on the night of October 16, 1934. They immediately began cutting their way through barbed wire strung by Chiang's troops, and blowing up blockhouses. Soon they had opened up a breach in the siege lines several miles wide. Within forty-eight hours, the main body of the Fourth Red Army and its civilian comrades poured through.

Because none of the 100,000 marchers knew exactly where they were going, none could possibly know what lay ahead. Perhaps it was just as well. If they had known, many might have turned back. For ahead lay a year-long trek of some 6,000 miles—more than twice the distance across the United States—through some of the most rugged and difficult country in the world. During their heroic journey, the marchers would endure incredible hardships. Some would die of starvation. Some would drown in icy rivers or swampy marshes. Others would freeze to death. Still others would fall before the guns of Chiang's Kuomintang military forces attacking both on the ground and from aircraft overhead. Only a relative handful of the marchers would survive this trial by fire. But many of those who did survive would one day rule China.

The "twenty-thousand-*li* march," as Mao usually referred to it—the Long March, as it became popularly known—had begun.

7

Mao Takes Command

The Fourth Red Army met with surprisingly little resistance during the breakout from its Jiangxi base and for several days thereafter. There were two reasons for this. First, Chiang and his generals did not know where such a breakout attempt might occur and thus could not concentrate their troops in any one place. Secondly, once the breakout took place, the Kuomintang expected the Red Army to head directly north and west toward Hunan Province, where the Communists who had been driven out of Changsha still had a small base.

It was generally agreed among the Communist Party leaders that the Fourth Red Army should indeed head for Hunan. Beyond that they had no immediate plans. At Mao's urging, however, General Zhu De agreed that the breakout forces should immediately head south and then west and finally north into Hunan. They also moved mainly at night so that Chiang's air force of several hundred planes could not spot them. But on the darkest nights the long columns had a tendency to get strung out, and many marchers lost track of those in front of them. To avoid this confusion, it was agreed some travel would be done during the day. Almost immediately they were spotted by Chiang's aerial reconnaissance planes.

Once Chiang was alerted to the general direction of the Red Army's movement, he ordered the Kuomintang to set up massive road blocks in southern Hunan. He also dispatched the main body of his troops to an area along the Xiang River, where he knew the Communists must cross to enter southern Hunan. It was at this point that the Red Army had its first major encounter and suffered its first serious losses.

There has been much disagreement over just how severe the Communist losses were in crossing the Xiang. Some estimates have ranged as high as 50,000 men—more than half of the Red Army forces; this seems improbable. But the losses were high indeed. The Kuomintang was entrenched along the river and had set up strong points at all bridges and places where the river was shallow enough to be forded. There was some discussion among the Reds about finding another crossing area, but the Communist top command, against Mao's advice, voted to proceed straight ahead with the attack.

The crossing took a week of brutal fighting. The river was literally red with blood; the shallows were choked with perhaps 30,000 Red Army corpses. The wounded were left to die in lonely agony, their mouths stuffed with clothing to stifle their screaming. Once the crossing was accomplished, Mao voiced his violent objections to the manner in which the entire Communist operation was being conducted. And the other Red leaders now began to pay more careful attention to his advice.

First of all, Mao pointed out, their operation had to be streamlined. Such unnecessary baggage as printing presses and large household items must be abandoned so the advancing columns could move more swiftly. They must also proceed only at night. Each person was ordered to tie a white towel to his or her pack, so that the person behind could see and follow more easily. Secondly, there should be not one single main column but several, and these columns should not travel in a straight line but zigzag across the countryside like ships in a wartime convoy. As it was, the Kuomintang could easily note the route of the advancing Red Army and then simply set up a blocking force in its path.

But Mao's most important suggestion—actually it was a demand—was that they abandon their plans to link up with the small Communist base in northern Hunan. Chiang was already massing his forces in front of them there, and to march head on into such a trap was suicidal. Instead, Mao suggested they should march farther west into Guizhou Province, where there were few Kuomintang forces. There they could capture the key city of Zunyi and perhaps link up with a small body of Communists who controlled a portion of Sichuan Province. Actually Mao was already planning on marching much farther north to join Jiangxi's sister soviet in Shaanxi Province, but he did not mention this at this time.

Mao's plan was accepted and in fact heartily approved of by General Zhu, who could not risk any further major troop losses. Within a matter of weeks, the city of Zunyi fell to the Communists. It did not fall by frontal assault, but by deception. Once again the ruse was suggested by Mao and carried out by General Zhu. Zhu's soldiers captured a village near

Zunyi that was occupied by Kuomintang troops. These troops were bribed into disclosing the details of how Zunyi was defended. Then they were stripped of their uniforms, which were put on by Zhu's troops. These disguised Red Army soldiers marched toward Zunyi at night, Little Red Devil buglers announcing their approach by playing Kuomintang bugle calls. The Reds then made their way past the Kuomintang guards at Zunyi, saying they had just returned from an attack on the Communists. Once inside the city they seized all of the key defensive posts at bayonet point, shouting, "We are the Workers' and Peasants' Red Army of China!" Little Red Devil bugle calls signaled the remainder of the Communists to enter the city.

When he received the startling news of the fall of Zunyi, Chiang Kai-shek flew to Kunming in Yunnan Province, and made plans to rally his forces in this area and drive the Reds out of southwest China. "The fate of the nation," Chiang announced, "depends on destroying the Red bandits south of the Yangtze River."

But in Zunyi the Reds were making their own plans. A meeting of the Political Bureau (Politburo) of the CCP Central Committee was called. This meeting was to be the most important meeting in CCP history. For the first time, both General Zhu De and top party functionary Chou En-lai spoke in favor of Mao Tsetung's taking complete charge of all Communist activities in China. Chou's switch in loyalties to Mao was prompted by the soundness of Mao's advice up to this point—without which, he pointed out, they would not have survived to reach Zunyi.

General Zhu said simply: "Everything Mao has told us to do up to now has been right. All other advice has been wrong."

Mao was elected head of the Politburo, the most powerful role in the CCP. Chou En-lai was elected his deputy. General Zhu remained in command of what was now known as the First Front Army, but his orders would come from Mao.

This was a turning point. Up to now the Long March had been simply an unguided mass movement across southern China. Now Mao was to supply the guidance as well as the inspiration and driving force without which the Long March never could have succeeded.

Mao told his comrades that from this point forward, the First Front Army would fight only as guerrillas. There would be no more head-on confrontations with Chiang's Kuomintang. And they would recruit new followers from the peasantry along the way.

This last announcement apparently severed the final ties with the Soviet Union, where Joseph Stalin was now in power. Stalin was strongly opposed to "peasant armies." Industrial workers were still the key to worldwide revolution, Stalin insisted, following strict Marxist doctrine.

But, Mao insisted, it was the Chinese peasants who could and should control China. It was the Chinese peasants who had suffered most at the hands of warlords and dictator emperors down the years. It was the peasants who had gone without food so frequently and so long that the traditional Chinese greeting was not "How are you?" but "Have you eaten?"

Mao, however, did not publicly announce any complete severance of the CCP's ties with Russia. He was still a confirmed Marxist and always would be. But of even greater importance, Mao, like many great political leaders, had a strong sense of self-preservation, especially insofar as his cause was concerned. He was now more determined than ever to march toward

China's northwest and join up with the other Chinese soviet in Shaanxi Province. And if they were successful in doing this, Mao reasoned, they would be relatively close to the Soviet Union and might obtain support from Stalin's vast armies.

Mao also knew that patriotism was a powerful weapon. He prepared to use that weapon now. The First Front Army and its civilian auxiliary remained in Zunyi for several weeks. During this time Mao made known his plans to march all the way to Shaanxi Province. But they would be marching there not merely to join up with their Shaanxi comrades, Mao pointed out. Nearby was Manchuria, where the hated Japanese invaders had now gained wide control. Playing on the patriotism of his followers, Mao coined a slogan that immediately became the Long March battle cry: "March north to fight the Japanese!"

The battle cry and the new "spirit of Zunyi," as it was called, were so contagious that by the time the Red Army was ready to resume its march, 4,000 local youths had been recruited from among the local population.

Mao's guerrilla tactics were immediately effective when the First Front Army left Zunyi in late January of 1935. To prevent the Reds from crossing the Yangtze, Chiang had placed 225,000 Kuomintang troops along the river on a one hundred-mile-wide front. But the Reds made no attempt at a frontal assault, as they had along the Xiang River. Instead, General Zhu sent a corps of men under Commander Lin Piao on a swift feint toward the southwest to attack Chiang's headquarters at Kunming. Chiang had word of this advance via radio—American field radios were supplied to Chiang's forces—and assumed it would take Lin Piao's troops a week to reach Kunming. But Lin Piao and his men literally ran the 125 miles toward their target. They reached Kunming in three days.

When Chiang, who had his wife with him at his headquarters, was informed that the Reds were at the city gates, he and his wife and aides fled the city by a railway that led into French Indochina (today's Vietnam). A few days later he received word by radio that the attack at Kunming, which was much smaller than had been first reported, had been beaten off. Chiang at once suspected the worst, that the attack on Kunming had merely been a diversionary effort and the main body of Red bandits was elsewhere.

Meanwhile, as Lin Piao and his men launched their attack on Kunming, General Zhu led his main body of the First Front Army to the upper reaches of the Yangtze beyond the area that was defended in depth by Chiang's Kuomintang forces. Here, at a point called the River of Golden Sands, the Red advance scouts seized several ferries and small boats and began ferrying some 50,000 Red troops across the river. The operation took several days. Beyond the river to the north there was deep forest, and by the time Chiang's troops had reacted and arrived on the scene, the Long Marchers had disappeared into the sanctuary of trees, leaving behind them the burning ferry boats. They also left behind on the north bank a small rear guard to greet Chiang's forces when they arrived on the river's south bank. "Come on across," the Red rear guard soldiers shouted cheerfully across the river, "the swimming's fine."

Chiang's troops shouted back futile threats. Then they set off on a 200-*li*-long march of their own upstream to find a suitable crossing. Meanwhile, the First Front Army was moving steadily north through the impenetrable forest where even Chiang's reconnaissance planes could not detect them.

When Chiang learned what had happened, he was furious. Immediately he flew into Sichuan Province, which the Long Marchers had now entered, and prepared to stop them at yet one more major river they must cross. This was the mighty Tatu, where the Reds would perform one of their most heroic feats during the Long March.

But before attempting to cross the Tatu River, the Reds were faced with a different kind of challenge. This was making their way through the formidable Land of the Lolos.

8

Through the Land of the Lolos

Lololand was a rugged mountainous area whose fierce aborigine tribesmen, the Black Lolos and White Lolos, had never been conquered by the Chinese. In fact Chinese armies had long avoided Lololand because few had ever passed through it without suffering severe losses. From time to time, however, the Kuomintang had raided and plundered the area, so the Lolos were justly suspicious of all Chinese soldiers.

Much of Lololand's forbidding nature was also due to its central physical feature, the Sikang Mountains. And to cross the Sikang Mountains it was necessary to climb the notorious Fire Mountain. Here no vegetation grew and there was no water, only jets of steam issuing from fissures in the rocks and from the dry streambeds. According to Chinese legend, the first monkeys that crossed Fire Mountain had all the hair on their bottoms burned off, and that is why monkeys have no hair on their bottoms today.

But Mao and his Long Marchers were not so concerned with conquering Fire Mountain as they were about coming to terms with the fierce Lolo tribesmen. And it was here that Mao's ideas about equal and fair treatment of all peasants as well as minorities bore their first fruit. Traditionally, whenever a Chinese army approached a village, especially in one of China's outlying provinces, the villagers fled in fright. It was usual for soldiers to seize whatever food, money, and private property and possessions they wanted. Even rape was not uncommon.

But Mao had already begun to educate the Red Army to serve the people. His so-called "Eight Points for Attention," issued to all Red Army units, indicated how Red soldiers were expected to act, in contrast to the customary Kuomintang soldiers' practice of loot, rape, and pillage. The Eight Points were:

1. Speak politely to the people. Don't hit or swear at them.
2. Pay fairly for what you buy.
3. Return everything you borrow.
4. Don't damage crops, but pay for anything you do damage.
5. Replace all doors and return all straw on which you sleep. [Doors on peasant huts were easily removable and used as beds at night.]
6. Dig latrines away from houses and fill them with earth when you leave.
7. Do not take liberties with women.
8. Do not mistreat captives.

These were supplemented by "Three Main Rules of Discipline," which were also rigidly enforced. They were:

1. Obey orders in all your actions.
2. Don't take a single needle or piece of thread from the masses.
3. Turn in everything captured.

More than one Red soldier was brought up short when he learned that these rules meant what they said—and that they applied to all ranks. One of Chou En-lai's aides, Wei Kuo-lu, for example, thought he would ingratiate himself with Chou by "liberating"—as G.I.s in World War II would call this practice—ten eggs and some cornmeal from a local farmer and presenting them to the Red Army Vice Chairman in the form of cornmeal mush. Chou was neither amused nor pleased. Since the eggs and cornmeal could not now be returned, Chou made his aide write a note of apology to the farmer and then return with it and some money to pay for what had been stolen. Chou also refused to eat the mush, insisting that it be divided among the rest of his staff.

The Lolos were extremely hostile when the Red Army first entered their territory, and there were numerous casualties. But when the Lolos found they were dealing with a new breed of Chinese soldier, they became more friendly. It was then that Mao played his trump card.

Mao had observed that there was a great rivalry between the Black Lolos and the White Lolos, but that it was the Black Lolos who actually ruled Lololand. He decided, therefore, to deal with the Black Lolos. Mao and his aides met with the Black Lolo leaders, and Mao pointed out that their rivalry with the White Lolos was similar to that between the Red Army and Chiang's "White" Kuomintang. All of the Lolos, Mao also knew, hated the Kuomintang for its raids into Lololand and its attempts to exploit and oppress the Lolos. The Reds too hated the Kuomintang, Mao said, because it was trying to exploit and oppress not only the Communists but also the whole of China. Mao then went on to speak of how, once the Kuomintang Nationalists were defeated, the Communists would divide all of China's lands among the peasants and minority groups such as the Lolos. Therefore it was only logical, Mao said, that the Lolos and the Reds join forces against the Kuomintang. Mao then proceeded to seal the bargain with a gift of silver money to the Black Lolo empress, and Mao's aides took part in a formal ceremony with the other Black Lolo leaders that included drinking from a bowl of chicken blood. This meant that the Blacks and the Reds were now blood brothers.

The Black Lolos were so impressed with Mao's inspirational message about Communist plans for China's future that they agreed to provide the Red Army with guides and guarantee the Reds a safe passage across Fire Mountain and through the rest of Lololand all the way to the Tatu River. Several hundred Black Lolos even joined the ranks of the Red Army and remained with it throughout the remainder of the Long March.

The Black Lolos also provided the Red Army with a certain amount of food, although they scarcely had enough for themselves. These welcome new supplies included rice, potatoes, pieces of pumpkin, pea and bean sprouts, and *chingko,* or barley cakes.

Chiang's forces had made no attempt to follow the Red Army into Lololand. Chiang himself assumed that the Reds would become embattled with the fierce Lolos and probably be destroyed. He was quite content to let the Lolos do the

Kuomintang's work of annihilating the Red bandits. But Chiang did send out occasional aerial reconnaissance missions. He also ordered his advance troops to guard two key crossings of the Tatu River, a ferryboat crossing at the village of Anshunchang and a suspension bridge farther upriver at Luting. The main body of his troops he stationed in southern Sichuan Province, within what he considered easy striking distance of the Tatu.

With the aid of their Lolo guides, the Reds had little difficulty crossing Fire Mountain. Once beyond the protection of the Sikang Mountains, however, the Long Marchers found themselves out in the open. Once again they traveled only by night, but they traveled swiftly, marching as much as seventy *li*, almost twenty-five miles, in a single night. By late May 1935 they had reached Anshunchang on the Tatu without detection.

The Tatu River ran generally north and south, but at this point it flowed east and west. The Red Army approached from the southwest, arriving at the crest of the ridge above the river's south bank at about ten P.M. on a dark, misty night. The Kuomintang advance guard was stationed in the main part of the village on the opposite or north bank. The guard numbered only about 800 men, but a squad of defenders would have been sufficient—save for one fatal error.

The Reds, exhausted from the last leg of their forced march, fell on their packs and slept. But Mao, General Zhu, and several other Red Army leaders lay on the crest of the ridge, staring down at the river through the light rain and trying to figure out how the river might be crossed that night. They knew that Anshunchang was a ferry crossing, but they also knew Chiang's guard would have moored all of the ferryboats on the opposite shore. Nevertheless, several scouts were sent down to the riverbank to search the near shore. Within an hour they had returned with startling news: a single ferryboat had been moored on *this* side of the river!

What the ferry was doing there no one bothered to ponder. Later it turned out that the garrison commander had friends and relatives on the south bank and, with apparently no enemy in the neighborhood, had seen no harm in an evening's visit.

The Reds quickly dispatched a crack unit of guerrillas, again led by Lin Piao, to capture the garrison commander, his guards, and, most important of all, the fifty-passenger ferry. This was accomplished—virtually without a sound—in less than an hour. The ferry was filled with more crack troops, those on the foredeck wearing the uniforms of the captured Kuomintang guard. And then it made for the far shore.

The Kuomintang garrison on the north bank was taken by complete surprise, and most of the men were fast asleep. Before dawn, the village of Anshunchang was in Red hands, along with its two additional ferries. Once the three ferries were returned to the south bank, the Reds immediately began to transport their troops and supplies across the river.

But it was a slow process—too slow, Mao and his aides soon decided. Spring rains had turned the Tatu into a raging torrent, wider and more turbulent than the Yangtze. It took several hours to make a single crossing, and by the end of several days only 5,000 men had been ferried across, even though the ferries were crowded with three times their normal passenger load. A number of Red soldiers had in fact been swept from the crowded ferryboat decks when the river rushed over the boats' sides, which were far too low in the water for safety. And Chiang's air force, finally alerted to the Reds' whereabouts, had also begun to bomb the crossing, causing numerous additional casualties. Mao had no doubt that the main body of Chiang's forces were marching toward the Tatu from the southeast.

Mao knew of the famous chain-link suspension bridge farther upstream. He had first learned about it in *The Romance of the Three Kingdoms,* one of the banned books that he and his classmates had read in primary school. General Zhu and Chou En-lai had also heard of the bridge. The three now decided to let Lin Piao and his men who had already crossed the river proceed to march north on one side of the river while the bulk of the Red Army marched on the other side. The two forces could again link up once the main body of Reds had crossed "the bridge built by Lu" or "The Bridge of Thirteen Chains."

Their decision was a desperate one. Mao recalled that it was here on the banks of the Tatu that the heroes of *The Romance of the Three Kingdoms* had met their defeat—and their deaths. He trusted this was not an ill omen. Crossing the Bridge of Thirteen Chains would be the Red Army's last chance to move into northern China. If they could not do so, they would probably have to return to Lololand, and the Long March would end in failure.

9

Crossing the Bridge of Thirteen Chains

The suspension bridge at Luting had been built many centuries earlier by an enterprising but otherwise relatively unknown local warlord named Lu Ting. After the bridge was in place Lu exacted tolls from anyone who wanted to cross it. After Lu's death the practice of collecting tolls was dropped, and the only currency needed to pay one's passage was courage.

The bridge had a span of about 100 yards (91.5 m). It stretched across the Tatu River, which boiled along its rocky course some 200 feet (61 m) below. The bridge consisted of thirteen hawserlike chains, each one several inches thick—or "thick as a rice bowl is round," as Mao later described them. On each side of the chasm the heavy iron chains were anchored beneath cemented piles of rocks. Four of the chains—two on each side of the walkway—served as hand- or guardrails. These were essential: as soon as anyone ventured onto the bridge it began to sway back and forth like a trapeze. The other nine chains supported the walkway, which was covered with thick wooden boards—or was until the Red Army arrived.

Once the decision was reached to make its main crossing of the Tatu at Luting, the First Front Army moved out rapidly. The distance to be covered was about two hundred miles (321 km), and most of it was through rugged mountain country. Since Chiang had already discovered them and there was no further purpose in concealment, the Reds marched day and night. They were certain Chiang would have an advance guard at the suspension bridge just as there had been at the ferry crossing. But the main Kuomintang force was still behind them. The most important thing for them now, all of the Red leaders agreed, was to keep out in front of the Kuomintang, cross the Tatu, and disappear yet once again into the forests and mountains beyond.

A forced march was difficult under the best of conditions. At night and in mountainous terrain, there were additional hazards. To light their way the Long Marchers lit torches made of dry reeds from the riverbank tied together in bundles and soaked in kerosene. One such torch was carried by each squad, whose members were told to follow its light closely. Often afterward those who had taken part in the Long March recalled the beauty of the light flickering from the thousands of torches and reflecting off the rocky canyon walls, making the moving column resemble a fiery dragon in the night.

But soon it began to rain, extinguishing most of the torches. Some marchers lost their way and fell silently to their deaths off the steep cliffs into the surrounding darkness.

Nevertheless, the Reds pushed on, resting at most only ten minutes out of every hour. They covered the last eighty miles (128 km) in twenty-four hours, arriving at Luting in the gray dawn of May 30, 1935.

From a military standpoint the suspension bridge at Luting should have been destroyed, and many of the Reds half expected this to have been done. But mainly because he did not want to antagonize the local populace—it would cost a great deal of money and take months to replace the bridge—Chiang had not ordered it destroyed. There before the somewhat unbelieving eyes of the exhausted Reds lay the Bridge of Thirteen Chains. But it was not intact.

To make crossing it virtually impossible, the Kuomintang had ripped up all of the bridge's floorboards on the Reds' side of the river. And on the opposite bank, at full combat alert, waited two regiments of several hundred Kuomintang troops. Most of them lay behind machine-gun emplacements protected by rock, with their weapons trained on the approaches to the bridge and the bridge itself.

Looking down into the deep gorge through which the Tatu River raged, the Reds knew they could never make their way down the sheer walls of the canyon to the riverbank. And if they could, there would be no way to ford the river. There was only one way to cross: the bridge must be taken. But how?

Mao and General Zhu decided to delay their assault on the bridge for a few hours. They were hopeful that Lin Piao and his Red troops who had crossed the river at Anshunchang would soon make their way to the suspension bridge on the opposite bank and launch a diversionary attack from there.

While Mao and his men waited, hidden behind their own rock barriers, the enemy shouted taunts at them across the chasm.

"Why don't you fly across? If you do, we promise to lay down our arms."

The Red soldiers shouted back, "We don't want your arms. It's your bridge we're after."

"Come and get it," came the reply.

By four o'clock in the afternoon the Red leaders decided to do just that.

Assault volunteers were called for. Twenty-two Red soldiers stepped forward. All were young. Most were still in their teens. None was older than twenty-five. All had Mauser rifles, knives, and grenades strapped to their backs. As they broke from cover and raced toward the bridge, their comrades laid down a heavy covering fire from rifles, machine guns, and mortars. But the enemy return fire was equally murderous.

The first volunteers to reach the bridge made no attempt to walk across on any of the chains that had supported the floorboards. Instead, they grasped the chains from beneath and swung out over the gorge. Hand over hand, they began to make their agonizingly slow way across the chasm. The human weights acted as pendulums, and the chains immediately began to sway back and forth, violently. The Reds thus became moving targets—more difficult to hit.

But soon enemy snipers began to find their targets. First one, then another, and another, and another Red volunteer was hit, to drop into the raging river below. Of the first twenty-two volunteers, only three made it to the other side.

But now there was no need to call for volunteers. As soon as a Red soldier was shot and dropped from the chains, half a dozen others ran forward to replace him in this hand-over-hand race against death.

Soon a spirit of wild hysteria seemed to have overcome the Reds. Several of them said later they suddenly felt they were no longer mortal, that nothing could stop them, that they could conquer any obstacle that stood before them. It was similar to the spirit that had swept through the ranks of Yankee soldiers at Lookout Mountain in the American Civil War. There it enabled the Yankees to race up the steep mountainside in the face of overwhelming Confederate fire and win a victory against impossible odds. Here the same spirit of abandon enabled the Chinese Red Army to conquer the enemy at the Bridge of Thirteen Chains.

When the Reds continued to swarm across the bridge hand over hand no matter how many of them were shot down, the Kuomintang soldiers began to experience their own form of hysteria: the hysteria of defeat. In a few moments, they realized, the Reds would reach the side of the bridge that still had floorboards on it.

In desperation the Kuomintang dumped kerosene on the remaining floorboards and set them afire.

The Reds were not to be denied. First one and then another and yet another reached the floored section of the bridge, climbed up through the flames, and began throwing hand grenades into the closely packed enemy. They raced forward, unslinging their rifles and firing into the machine-gun emplacements as they ran. Dozens of their comrades followed. Soon, a frenzy of hand-to-hand fighting began.

Meanwhile, on the Reds' side of the river, Mao had ordered numerous trees cut down and trimmed quickly into logs. As soon as the first handful of Reds reached the far bank, Mao ordered the logs dragged onto the bridge to replace the missing floorboards. As soon as these were in place, the main body of the Red Army poured across the bridge.

The two regiments of Kuomintang defenders did not wait for the full force of the Red attackers to hit them. They managed to free themselves from the hand-to-hand struggle and retreat—in a disorganized rout.

The Reds did not immediately pursue them. Instead, they consolidated their forces on what had been the Kuomintang side of the river, held memorial services for the dead, and awaited the arrival of Lin Piao.

That night the Reds were amazed when some of the Kuomintang soldiers who had fled from defending the bridge returned to the scene and volunteered to join the First Front Army. They did so either because they feared Chiang's wrath at their defeat or because they were impressed with the Reds' courage and dedication to their cause. Whatever their reasons for volunteering, Mao accepted them. The rest of the Kuomintang who had fled, Mao left to Chiang's tender mercies when he should arrive on the scene.

Lin Piao and his troops arrived the next day. They had had to fight several skirmishes with small detachments of Kuomintang troops but had dispersed them with few losses to themselves.

The Reds then removed all of the tree trunks and remaining scorched floorboards from the bridge so it could not be readily crossed by Chiang's main force. And there was little doubt that those forces soon would arrive. Chiang's airplanes were already circling overhead. The Red conquerors of the Bridge of Thirteen Chains took great delight in shaking their fists at the planes' pilots—a gesture similar in intent to thumbing their noses at the enemy.

Mao and the other Party leaders then held a council meeting to decide which route they should next follow. There was also little doubt that Chiang would now fill the western area of Sichuan Province with his best troops to prevent the Reds from continuing their heroic trek north. A route must be found around the Kuomintang blockade.

The only alternative seemed to be to leave China and somehow find a route through a section of eastern Tibet. But this was an area completely unknown to any of the Reds and occupied by an alien, warlike people called the Fan. It would also mean crossing a section of the Himalayas known as the Great Snowy Mountains, mountains that rose to an altitude of some 17,000 feet.

Among the Lolos who had joined the Reds there were several who had been in this part of Tibet and at least knew their way through the mountain passes. With the aid of these volunteer Lolo guides, Mao and his Long Marchers decided to assault the fortress of the Fan, the Great Snowy Mountains.

10

Crossing the Great Snowy Mountains

Chou En-lai's aide, Wei Kuo-lu, was just one among many of those on the Long March who always afterward said crossing the Great Snowy Mountains was the most difficult part of their entire journey. Many of the marchers, Wei said, feared entering this strange, seemingly impassable region. They had heard tales of this "weird place with its so-called 'magic mountains' that were so high that even the birds could not fly over them."

Even before they got to the mountains, the marchers had to make their way through heavily forested foothills. Here the huge virgin trees were so thick and tall that sunlight rarely reached the wet ground beneath them. Rain always seemed to be falling. The forest paths were knee-deep in slippery decaying leaves, making walking doubly difficult. Finding a dry place to sleep was all but impossible. Most of the marchers simply slept in the mud or leaning against trees.

Occasionally mountain goats or wild boars would be frightened from their hiding places by the marchers. These the soldiers tried to shoot, to add to their meager food supplies. In the village of Luting near the Bridge of Thirteen Chains they had managed to buy a limited quantity of ground corn as well as smaller amounts of rice, potatoes, and dried pumpkins. This food would have to sustain them in the weeks ahead. The rain supplied abundant drinking water. This was fortunate because the June heat was intense.

Soon, however, the marchers had reached the mountains' timberline, and temperatures began to drop as the elevation rose. The forest fell behind them, and they found themselves in open, rocky country. Ahead lay the mountains, their sides thick, solid blocks of ice and snow, their rampartlike peaks hidden in the clouds.

Steady precipitation fell from the leaden skies, not as rain but in the form of hailstones as large as walnuts or small potatoes. Unprotected by the trees, the marchers were beaten bloody by the hammering hail.

Most of the marchers were from southern China and had never experienced cold such as that in the Snowy Mountains. In addition, their clothing was lightweight cotton that was quickly penetrated by the cold. Nevertheless, the surviving soldiers, party officials, women, children, and pack animals pushed on. But now, for the first time, some of the soldiers began to voice their doubts about the wisdom of having civilians with them. Caring for them only increased the soldiers' difficulties and the delay. These doubts seemed to be confirmed when a halt had to be called for one of the women to give birth to a baby boy. The birth took place in a deep crevice in the snow where there was some protection from the wind but none from the cold. Miraculously, both mother and child survived the Long March.

Mao's wife, Ho Tzu-chen, had given birth to a baby daughter earlier in the march, although records do not indicate where along the way the birth occurred. Ho Tzu-chen had also been wounded by shrapnel in one of the Kuomintang attacks, but she and her baby also survived to reach Shaanxi.

While crossing the Snowy Mountains Mao himself became ill for a brief period with another of his recurring attacks of malaria. Mao, however, steadfastly refused to ride one of the pack animals despite the insistence of Chou En-lai and Chou's aide, and in a few days he was again well.

It was Mao whose indomitable spirit kept the Long Marchers moving. He traveled back and forth along the caravan, visiting with various dispirited groups, telling them stories, reciting his own patriotic poems, and urging them on with revolutionary slogans. On the backs of several of the pack animals Mao had also cached secret stores of hot peppers and ginger. Now he had the soldiers build fires and make a hot brew from the chilies and ginger, which was distributed to all of the marchers, raising both their temperatures and their spirits. Mao also joked about good, fiery peppers making good, fiery revolutionaries.

Most of the time, however, it was impossible to find fuel for fires, and food was mostly eaten raw. Something was wrong with the corn they had bought in Luting, and eating it upset most of the marchers' stomachs. A watery gruel made from mixing ground rice kernels with snow was the common fare.

As the trek through the Snowy Mountains wore on for days

and then weeks, some marchers began to doubt the guides. This mild form of paranoia was partially brought about by the cold and the high altitudes. Other forms of mental disturbances and sheer physical exhaustion struck some of the marchers, many of whom simply fell down in the snow muttering incoherently, never to rise again.

To make matters worse, as the marchers moved through the mountain passes, the native Fan tribesmen rolled huge boulders down on them to protest the Reds' intrusion into Fan territory. Mao had no opportunity to meet with and persuade the Fan people to become the Reds' allies as he had done with the Lolos. The Fan tribesmen remained hidden and inaccessible in their remote eyries, guarding the land they called "The Roof of the World."

By July, when the Long Marchers began to stumble down out of the mountains and head toward the plain that was the northwest corner of Sichuan, their number had dwindled to some 25,000 men, women, and children.

As they moved through one final mountain pass on their way back into their native China, one final rock was hurled into the Reds' midst. But this rock was not hurled by the Fan. It had a message wrapped around it that read:

"We are Zhang Guotao's Red Army troops. Our headquarters are forty *li* ahead at Inien."

At first it was thought these might be Communist troops from the sister soviet at Shaanxi that was the goal of the Long Marchers. But the Shaanxi soviet was still too far away for troops to have been sent out from there to meet them. Whoever they were, Mao's soldiers were delighted at long last to have encountered not enemies but apparently allies. But Mao himself was not so enthusiastic. He knew who Zhang Guotao was, and he looked forward to their meeting once again with many reservations.

Mao had not seen Zhang for many years. They had been young Red revolutionaries together back in their student days. And both had joined in the founding of the Communist Party in 1921. Since then Mao had pretty much lost track of Zhang, whom he remembered as a strict, Russian-oriented Communist. Zhang had opposed Mao's peasant-oriented ideas of Chinese revolution, favoring instead the traditional Marxist views that the industrial workers in the cities must be the true Red revolutionaries. When Chiang had suddenly turned on the Communists and set out on a systematic campaign to annihilate them, Zhang and some of his followers had gone into hiding in Sichuan Province. There they had begun to build up an army of their own. Mao had heard of Zhang's army, but he had also heard disturbing reports that Zhang was no longer a true Communist revolutionary but now had ideas of becoming at least an important Chinese warlord and at most the future ruler of China.

But Zhang was still very much a self-proclaimed Red revolutionary when he and Mao met again at Inien. He greeted Mao warmly. Yet when Zhang was informed that Mao was now Chairman of the Chinese Communist Party, Zhang objected strongly. How could the decision at Zunyi making Mao head of the Politburo be valid when all the leading Communists were not there? He, Zhang, had not been there, and he was a charter member of the Communist Central Committee. No, Zhang insisted, Mao was not Party Chairman but simply a guerrilla leader. And Communist Party doctrine was firmly against guerrillaism.

For a time Mao and Chou En-lai and their fellow Party

officials feared that Zhang's objections to Mao's new status might lead to open conflict between the two Red armies. They grew even more apprehensive when they realized that their own military commander, General Zhu De, apparently sided with Zhang. Why General Zhu's sudden shift in allegiance occurred was not then or afterward made clear. Perhaps General Zhu harbored some resentment over having to take orders from a civilian commander like Mao. Or perhaps he just thought Zhang would eventually command the winning side. There was little doubt that General Zhu was impressed with the size and physical condition of Zhang's Red army. It outnumbered the Long Marchers' bedraggled and exhausted forces by at least 10,000 men, and they all seemed to be well equipped and in top physical condition.

Mao, of course, was realist enough to know that a civil war between his own force and Zhang's must be avoided even if it meant the loss of General Zhu. Mao suggested that they simply all march together to the Northwest and Shaanxi Province, with each army maintaining its own separate identity. But Zhang was opposed to marching to the Northwest at all. What was the point in doing that? Shaanxi was a backwater with no future and few well-trained troops, Zhang insisted, and the idea of fighting against the Japanese was simply so much opium smoke. Why shouldn't they all join forces here and now, march westward into Tibet, and there establish a major base from which they could eventually challenge Chiang's Kuomintang? Or perhaps they could simply remain where they were and work out a compromise peace with Chiang. This last point Zhang only hinted at, and claimed he had been misunderstood when he was told he sounded like a traitor. And as far as Tibet was concerned, the Long Marchers made it quite clear that none of them wanted to hear anything more about that icy wasteland.

Mao was now certain that his earlier suspicions were correct. Zhang was not so much interested in promoting the Communist cause for the good of the people of China as he was interested in promoting the Zhang cause for his own good. Once in Tibet, Mao also felt certain, he and his First Front Army comrades would be overwhelmed by Zhang's followers, and that would be an end to the Communist cause in China.

When this debate had continued fruitlessly for several days, word was received of the approach of Kuomintang troops. The Reds abandoned their discussions long enough to beat off advance units of the Kuomintang, and then, suddenly and surprisingly, Zhang gave up his opposition to marching toward Shaanxi Province. As Mao had suggested, however, they would do so as two separate armies. To this Mao agreed, despite the fact that the agreement also included the provision that General Zhu would join Zhang's forces as military commander.

The two groups started out together toward the area known as the Great Grasslands. This swampy region was the last major physical barrier between the Reds and the soviet in Shaanxi Province. But the two groups did not long remain together. Soon Zhang suggested that to avoid pursuit they should follow different routes. Since this was in keeping with his own guerrilla tactics, Mao could not object.

When the groups split up, the agreement was that they would rejoin beyond the Great Grasslands. But Mao and his Long Marchers never saw Zhang and General Zhu's army again. Later Zhang was to claim that they had encountered a strong force of Kuomintang and fighting them off had prevented them from keeping the rendezvous. General Zhu, on the other hand, claimed that they had been unable to ford a river in flood and had had to turn back, thus preventing the agreed-upon meeting. Mao himself always kept a discreet silence on the subject, his only observation being the somewhat wry one that whatever Zhang's and Zhu's reasons for failing to keep to their original agreement, they had somehow managed to get into Tibet—where Zhang had originally suggested they go.

This was true. Zhang attempted to set up a major base in eastern Tibet, from which he planned to make a bid for the leadership of China. But this bid was to end in failure, and a year later Zhang and General Zhu sheepishly made their way back to Mao at Shaanxi. With them was only a handful of troops, all the rest of their once-proud and powerful army having been destroyed by Chiang's Kuomintang. Mao successfully defended both men against the accusation of desertion made by the Long Marchers. In General Zhu's case, Mao's faith proved justified. Zhu went on to successfully command all of the Red armies in the victorious fight against Japan. Zhang, however, eventually defected to the Kuomintang and became a spy against the Reds. He was to gain an undying reputation as an arch traitor and be regarded in the same light by the Communist revolutionaries as Benedict Arnold was by the American revolutionaries.

Meanwhile, the Long Marchers under Mao and Chou En-lai had to make their own way across the Great Grasslands.

11

Crossing the
Great Grasslands

Like the Great Snowy Mountains, the Great Grasslands were occupied by a hostile people. The Grasslands people were called the Man, and their queen had long had a standing rule: she would boil alive any of her subjects who helped intruders into Man territory. As a result, for the first time during the Long March Mao had to allow his troops to steal food from the local populace. Otherwise they would have starved or been forced to survive wholly on boiled pinecones, tree bark, and marsh grass. But Mao vowed that one day the Reds would repay the Man for the food they had stolen from them.

In some ways food was the least of the Long Marchers' worries in crossing the Great Grasslands. Far more formidable were the terrain itself and the unpredictable weather. The Grasslands were actually a vast, upland swamp. Fierce winds from the Himalayas swept down across this swamp, bringing driving rainstorms one day and snowstorms the next. The grass in the swamp grew to shoulder height and was as thick as jungle undergrowth. Its only advantage was that it could be used to make crude thatched huts for shelter from the most severe storms.

There was no consistently solid ground in the Grasslands, only islandlike hummocks of spongy earth that could support just a few people at a time. This made it impossible for the Long Marchers to travel in columns. They had to break up into small groups, with each individual jumping from hummock to hummock. Missteps often resulted in death by drowning or suffocation in the gluey mud. This mud acted like quicksand. Anyone falling into it had to be quickly pulled out to avoid being sucked down into its thick, foul-smelling depths. Hundreds died in this fashion.

Obtaining guides to cross the Grasslands was a major problem. In the forests the marchers passed through before actually entering the swamp itself, attempts were made to enlist the aid of the Man warriors as guides. When all such attempts ended in failure—"Each attempt to buy a sheep or enlist a guide cost the life of at least one man," Mao later stated— Mao authorized his soldiers to capture a number of Man tribesmen and force them into service with the Reds. This was done, and the captives led the way through the Grasslands at bayonet point. There was some doubt, of course, about how trustworthy the captive Man guides might be, but the Red soldiers made it clear to them that any treachery would result in their being drowned in the mud of their native swamp. In the end the Man guides proved wholly trustworthy, and several of them later chose to continue with the Reds to their destination.

Whether they did so out of conversion to the Red cause or from fear of being boiled alive if they returned to their homeland was never wholly clear.

The Long Marchers started through the Great Grasslands in mid-August 1935. With General Zhu gone, Lin Piao was the acting military commander, and he and his soldiers with their Man guides led the way. Strung out behind Lin Piao's military vanguard the rest of the Long Marchers followed, guided by a long, horsehair rope the soldiers had stretched across the tops of the reeds as a trail marker. As soon as they were well into the swamp they were attacked by huge mosquitoes as big as horseflies. Bites from these monster mosquitoes resulted in a particularly virulent fever called "black malaria," and within a few days several hundred marchers had succumbed to this disease. Fortunately, the weather changed suddenly and an Arctic-like blast of freezing wind from the Himalayas killed the mosquitoes. But the arctic wind was also accompanied by snow, blinding the marchers and halting their progress for several days. On the largest hummocks reed huts were hastily built, and these helped the marchers weather the gale. But when the storm subsided, dozens of bodies were found frozen to death on hummocks too small to support a shelter. Among the dead were several Little Red Devil buglers. Their loss was an especially severe blow to the marchers. In a rough, simple, yet moving ceremony, the boys' bodies were committed to the black waters of the swamp.

Once the march was resumed, the food situation became desperate. Most of the meager supply of ground wheat and barley that had been stolen earlier was now gone, leaving little to eat but the marsh grass itself. Some marchers took to digging up the roots of other swamp plants and eating them, but many of these wild bulbs proved to be poisonous. For the first time Mao had to authorize the slaughter of pack animals, and those few animals that had not already drowned in the mud were now killed and eaten by the marchers. This desperate measure was probably the only thing that made it possible for the trek to continue.

Finally, in late September, the ordeal of the Great Grasslands came to an end. The shoulder-high grasses and reeds now began to reach only to the marchers' knees. Underfoot there was once again firm ground. And then, at long last, they were again out in the open, free to march in columns as the First Front Army. Ahead lay the windswept plains of Kansu Province, the last province between the Long Marchers and their goal of Shaanxi.

But also ahead lay a solid phalanx of Kuomintang troops.

Chiang had sent out reconnaissance aircraft to follow the Red Army's progress through the Grasslands. Once the Reds emerged from the swamp, he planned to have his troops ready and waiting to deliver the final blow to the exhausted survivors.

But Mao and his aides had no intention of engaging in any final showdown with the Kuomintang. To do so could only result in the total destruction of the First Front Army. Instead Mao sent a part of his forces in a feint toward Outer Mongolia, where it would appear the Reds were trying to make contact with the Russian military command known to be in that area. Mao ordered these diversionary Red forces to move out in broad daylight so that Chiang would have no doubt about the direction of their movement. But the bulk of the Red forces Mao held in reserve until nightfall. Then they started their march across Kansu Province, toward Shaanxi. The diversionary forces were told to march toward Outer Mongolia during the first day, but that night to double back and rejoin the main body of the First Front Army. This would mean twenty-four hours of virtually nonstop marching. But Lin Piao, who was to head this movement, assured Mao that his men were up to the effort.

Chiang and the Kuomintang were completely fooled by the feint. Perhaps they were ready to be fooled because Outer Mongolia was where Chiang had always suspected the First Front Army was headed; in fact, he had already sent some forces ahead to guard the Mongolian border. As soon as the Reds moved out, Chiang ordered the rest of the Kuomintang toward Mongolia. Now, he was certain, the final confrontation with Mao's Red bandits would occur. It was several days before he became aware of his major blunder.

But the First Front Army was not yet home free. Kansu Province was occupied by hostile Moslem troops, who tried to prevent the Reds from marching through their province. Nearness to their final goal and the memory of the all but unbearable hardships they had gone through to get this far drove the Reds into a wild frenzy. Already driven to the limits of human endurance, the Red Army troops somehow summoned up new reserves of energy. They attacked with a fury the Moslems had rarely seen, even managing to break up a Moslem cavalry attack and capture most of the cavalry horses. These animals were used to carry the sick and wounded. After the Moslem defense was broken, the First Front Army, which had been successfully rejoined by Lin Piao and his men, had to engage in only a few minor skirmishes the rest of the way across Kansu Province.

As the Reds neared their goal, a fierce-looking band of mounted soldiers rode out to meet them. Mao feared that this was yet another troop of Moslem cavalry. But then he recognized that their leader was another old friend from his student revolutionary days, Liu Chih-tan.

Liu Chih-tan was the commander of the Communist soviet at Shaanxi. This soviet had been established at the time Chiang Kai-shek and his Kuomintang had turned on the Communists and commenced his series of campaigns to annihilate them. Because it was in such an out-of-the-way area of China, Chiang had largely ignored it. Consequently, Lin Chih-tan and his compact but well-trained little army of less than 10,000 men had to defend their soviet only against attacks from local warlords. This they had successfully done on several occasions, so they were battle-tested soldiers.

Now Liu Chih-tan dismounted and ran forward to greet Mao. Throwing his arms around the Chairman, Liu said, "Long live the Communist Party! Together we can conquer the Kuomintang."

The date was October 20, 1935. A year after it had begun in Jiangxi, the Long March was ended.

There were those among the Long Marchers, including Chairman Mao, who wept at the warmth of their reception from Liu and Liu's people. That night, for the first time in months, Mao slept with a roof over his head. His bedroom was a cave in the hills, but it was warm and dry—and safe. Before going to sleep Mao took time to write down a few of his thoughts. They accurately summed up the situation, and hinted at the future.

Of the 100,000 men, women, and children who had started from Jiangxi, only about 15,000 survivors had marched into Shaanxi in the shadow of the Great Wall. Just half of the Little Red Devils had lived to complete the march. But among the women, thirty out of the original thirty-five had survived. Most important of all, Mao noted, was the fact that the core of the First Front Army was still intact, and its morale and sense of political purpose were stronger than ever. Then Chairman Mao wrote, "Our Red Army is like a great tree that has been through a storm. It has lost some of its branches, but the trunk and roots are still intact."

Although Mao was not fully aware of it at this time, the epic Long March had accomplished something else. It had created a legend of indestructibility around the Red Army and its leaders that would stand them in good stead in the severe trials that lay ahead.

There was not long to wait for the first of these trials. Within a month a frustrated Chiang Kai-shek sent 60,000 Kuomintang troops into the dusty yellow hills surrounding the Shaanxi soviet in an all-out attempt to destroy the newly combined Red forces.

Stretching for over 1,500 miles across northern China, the Great Wall is regarded as one of the man-made wonders of the world. It was built over successive centuries beginning in the third century to keep out barbarians from the north. This picture was taken at a point known as Nankon Pass. *The Bettmann Archive*

Site of the Zunyi Conference, where, in January 1935, Mao Tsetung's leadership of the Chinese Communist Party was established. *US-China Peoples Friendship Association*

The Bridge of Thirteen Chains, spanning the Tatu River at the town of Luting. Kuomintang troops ripped up the thick wooden floorboards on the western side before Mao's First Front Army arrived there in May 1935. *Eastfoto*

Long Marchers climbing Chia-chin Mountain, one of the Great Snowy Mountains in Tibet. *Eastfoto*

About a month after leading the Long Marchers to their goal in Shaanxi province, Mao rides horseback in northern Shaanxi. Accompanying him are his wife, Ho Tzu-chen (behind him, wearing a broad-brimmed hat), and several Red Army soldiers. *Eastfoto*

Some weeks after the March, Mao talks with a Shaanxi peasant. One of the famous loess, or clay, hills is in the background. *US-China Peoples Friendship Association*

Several months after the March, Mao is shown in Yenan with two of the
Little Red Devils. *Monthly Review Press*

12

The Capture of Chiang Kai-shek

The Shaanxi soviet was an ideal stronghold against mass attack. Situated in a region of high hills, it had to be approached through a series of valleys so narrow that only a few men at a time could march through them abreast. The hills themselves were also ideal for defensive purposes. They were composed of a powdery yellow soil called loess, which over the centuries had blown down into China from the Gobi desert. This soil was soft enough so that caves could easily be dug into the faces of the hills, yet firm enough so that the caves could withstand the shock of artillery and mortar shells falling nearby. The Reds had dug many of these caves above the valley routes that an approaching enemy would have to take to enter the stronghold. From these caves the Reds could fire down on the enemy virtually without risk to themselves.

The Kuomintang quickly moved into this murderous maze of valleys—and almost as quickly moved out again, its number sorely depleted. Urged on by Chiang Kai-shek and his commanders, the Kuomintang repeated its futile attacks several more times with equal lack of success. In fact it was almost immediately clear that Chiang's sixth campaign to annihilate the Red bandits was going to be just as unsuccessful as the previous five had been.

After several weeks of these suicidal attempts to breach the Red Shaanxi stronghold, Chiang allowed his troops to retreat to the town of Sian, several hundred miles away. Here Chiang planned to build up the Kuomintang forces with reinforcements from throughout China and then have yet one more go at the Reds. This time, he vowed, he would overwhelm them with sheer numbers. He also planned to use bombing planes on the cave-infested hills. Meanwhile, Chiang flew back to Nanking, which was now the Nationalist capital. Japan, having completely consolidated its gains in Manchuria, had sent peace envoys to Nanking to meet with Chiang and his government. More than anything else, Chiang wanted to end the Japanese threat to his country so he could concentrate on exterminating the Reds, whom he regarded as China's number-one enemy.

Many Chinese, however, including large numbers of Chiang's own Nationalists, did not agree with Chiang. They wanted the hated Japanese driven out of the country and thought the Kuomintang should make that its main goal—even if this meant making peace with the Reds. Among those who thought so was a colorful young Kuomintang officer stationed at Sian named Chang Xueh-liang, but generally known as "The Young Marshal."

The Young Marshal was the son of a warlord who had controlled much of Manchuria. Driven out of Manchuria by the Japanese, the Young Marshal and several thousand of his troops had moved south, joined forces with the Kuomintang, and fought several battles against the Reds. But now he thought a continuation of the civil war would destroy China and allow Japan to simply march in and take over the entire country. The Young Marshal sent secret messages to Chairman Mao expressing his views and even allowed some of his soldiers to join the Red forces.

Mao had been thinking along the same lines as the Young Marshal for some time. The main enemy was Japan, and the only way Japan could be defeated was for the Red Army and the Kuomintang Army to mount a joint effort against the Japanese in Manchuria. But when Mao first presented this idea of a united front to the Communist Party Central Committee, it was met by violent opposition. Nevertheless, Mao persisted, pointing out to his comrades that there was little point in making plans for the future of Chinese Communism "if we are robbed of a country in which to practice it."

Within a few months Chairman Mao moved his headquarters to the town of Paoan in Shaanxi Province. Later he would again move, this time to the larger town of Yenan, as his forces began to grow in number and the Kuomintang no longer presented an immediate threat. Here Chairman Mao would spend the next ten years, directing the Red efforts, first, to defeat the Japanese and, finally, to defeat the Kuomintang and gain control of China.

Once Mao's forces were firmly established in Shaanxi Province, Red reinforcements began to flow in from throughout China. These were mostly small military units that had scattered throughout the country to avoid destruction by the Kuomintang. Soon Mao's Red Army and its auxiliary of women and children would swell to more than 100,000 and continue to grow. This shift in Communist power from south China to north China was to be of key importance in future events.

Meanwhile, Chiang Kai-shek, in Nanking, became impatient at the failure of his forces in Sian to mount an offensive against the Reds. Chiang had increased the size of the Sian garrison to some 300,000 men, but still the Kuomintang did not attack. When queried about the cause of this delay, Chiang's officers in Sian, among them the Young Marshal, Chang Xueh-liang, responded with a series of lame excuses. Finally Chiang decided to fly back to Sian and find out for himself what was wrong. The peace talks with Japan had now ended in failure, but Chiang still thought of the Reds as China's number-one enemy.

Chiang arrived in Sian in early December of 1936, and shortly thereafter the opening act of a bizarre drama began. He was quartered at a luxurious health resort outside the city where for centuries wealthy Chinese had come to take baths in the thermal springs. On the evening of December 11 Chiang himself took a bath in one of the hot mineral springs and then went to bed early. The next morning he was awakened equally early by an aide who said that the building was besieged by mutinous Kuomintang troops and that Chiang must escape or be killed.

Leaving in such haste that he only had time to don a bathrobe, Chiang fled in his bare feet and without his false teeth. The aide helped Chiang across the unguarded rear courtyard to a high wall. The aide also helped Chiang scale this wall, but in dropping to the ground on the far side Chiang wrenched his back. The aide helped him climb a nearby slope, but soon Chiang refused to go any farther.

What kind of an impression would it make on the Chinese people, Chiang demanded of his aide, for their barefoot leader to be captured running away clad only in his bathrobe and without his false teeth? And anyway, the rough ground hurt his bare feet. Chiang sat down on a log and refused to budge. "They can shoot me right here," he said.

Within a short time a squad of troops did arrive on the scene, and Chiang repeated his request that he be shot on the spot. Instead, the soldiers bundled him into a waiting automobile, sped with their prisoner into Sian, and lodged him in a jail cell. There he was greeted by the Young Marshal. Chiang at first refused to talk with him or any of his captors. But when they brought him his uniform, his shoes, and his false teeth, Chiang said he would at least listen to what they had to say.

The Young Marshal handed Chiang a piece of paper. On it were written several demands, the two most important calling on Chiang to end the civil war and form a united front with the Reds to fight the Japanese. These demands, the Young Marshal told Chiang, had already been forwarded to the Nationalist government in Nanking, along with the announcement that Chiang was being held in Sian until they were agreed to.

Chiang wadded up the paper into a ball and threw it on the floor.

The news that Chiang was being "detained" in Sian—the Young Marshal avoided using the term "prisoner" just as he denied a mutiny had occurred—hit like a bombshell both in Nanking and at Red Army headquarters in Paoan. It also made world news when it was picked up by newspaper and radio wire services.

When word of Chiang's capture reached the Soviet Union, Joseph Stalin assumed that either the Japanese or the Chinese Reds, probably the latter, were responsible. Stalin believed that Chiang was the only person with enough power to control China, and that his overthrow would create ungovernable chaos in the country. He feared that such a situation might also encourage the Japanese to make an all-out bid to take over China. Stalin still strongly favored the Chinese Reds' working with the Nationalist Kuomintang until the Reds had rebuilt their forces and could safely challenge Chiang and the Nationalists. The Soviet leader sent a radio message to Chairman Mao insisting that if the Reds had indeed captured Chiang, they must release him immediately.

Stalin's message made Chairman Mao literally hopping mad. After he received it, Mao jumped up and down in anger, swearing he would never again have anything to do with the Soviet Union in general and Joseph Stalin in particular. The thing that angered Mao most was the fact that the Russians had had little or nothing to do with Mao and his people while they were suffering the trials of the Long March, but now that the Reds showed new signs of strength, Stalin's interest in them had also revived. The Soviet leader, Mao concluded yet once again, was indeed a fair-weather friend.

Instead of replying to Stalin's message, Chairman Mao decided to send his aide, Chou En-lai, to confer with Chiang in Sian to see if the Nationalist leader was willing to listen to reason about the possibility of working out some sort of agreement with the Reds.

Meanwhile, there had been panic and confusion at Kuomintang headquarters in Nanking. No one in the Nationalist government knew exactly what to do about their leader Chiang being "detained" in Sian. No one, that is, except Chiang's wife, Madame Chiang Kai-shek. She was highly indignant about the disgraceful treatment of her husband at the hands of a few of his own disloyal troops. She was also determined to do something about it. Madame Chiang decided to fly to Sian and join her husband.

Madame Chiang was a woman with a shrewd political sense as well as a keen sense of history. She had demonstrated both back in the 1920s when she had married Chiang, who was then the new leader of the struggling Nationalists. Her maiden name had been Soong Meiling. She was one of the three famous Soong sisters, all of whom were noted for their beauty far beyond the borders of their native city of Shanghai. Meiling was a devout Christian in a family of Christians. She had gone to school in the United States for ten years, graduating from Wellesley College. After returning to China in 1927, she had been courted by the young Chiang. Her widowed mother objected to the marriage, just as she had successfully objected earlier to the courting of another Soong sister by the aging Sun Yat-sen. But this time she was not successful. Soong Meiling saw in Chiang the future leader of China and insisted on the marriage. When Chiang agreed to become a Christian, Soong Meiling's mother consented.

The marriage of the rapidly rising young army man from China's Whampoa Military Academy to one of the three much-sought-after Soong sisters had made news in the United States as well as in China. The fact that she was a Wellesley graduate was emphasized, as was Chiang's conversion to Christianity. Since then Madame Chiang had carefully cultivated foreign newsmen, especially Americans, on her husband's behalf, and news about him was sympathetically received abroad, especially in the United States. Most Americans were too preoccupied with the severe economic depression that gripped the country during the 1930s to know, or care, much about what was happening in China. But when the civil war began there between the Chinese Nationalists and the Reds, most Americans automatically knew they were on the side of the Christian Chiang's Kuomintang and against the atheistic Red Communists. Almost no Americans were aware of Mao Tsetung or any other Red leaders until long after the Long March.

Madame Chiang knew now that despite the Chinese government's attempts to suppress the news, word of Chiang's capture had already been flashed to the world's press. She also knew that the news that she had decided to join her husband in captivity was apt to make world headlines. Madame Chiang was seldom wrong in judging the pulse of publicity, and she was not wrong this time. Her flight to Chiang's side was the romantic stuff that reporters' and headline writers' dreams are made of.

By this time the Young Marshal in Sian realized he had indeed stirred up a hornet's nest when he and his mutinous troops had kidnapped Chiang. Chinese public opinion had favored Chiang's taking a firmer position against the Japanese, but it did not favor Chiang's being kidnapped and blackmailed into doing so. In fact most Chinese, including many Communist sympathizers, rallied to Chiang's cause and demanded his immediate release.

Seeking a satisfactory solution to the problem he had created, the Young Marshal welcomed Madame Chiang to Sian and encouraged her to sit in on the talks her husband was having with the Reds' envoy, Chou En-lai.

Mao had chosen well when he selected Chou En-lai to meet with Chiang. In fact Chou was probably the only Red leader Chiang would have consented to talk with. He remembered Chou favorably from his Whampoa Military Academy days and had never been able to understand how Chou had become an aide to the Red bandit leader Mao Tsetung. Chiang also scarcely recognized Chou at first because he had grown a beard and lost so much weight from the rigors of the Long March.

It was in these meetings with Chiang that Chou En-lai performed perhaps his greatest service not only to the Red cause but also to the whole Chinese people. Historians have agreed that the united front that grew out of these talks eventually saved China. Yet neither Chiang nor his wife, either then or later, ever acknowledged the importance of Chou's role at Sian.

Addressing Chiang as "Commandant," a flattering title that recalled their Whampoa Military Academy days, Chou pointed out that a continuing civil war between the Kuomintang and the Reds could destroy China. Already the Japanese were massing troops in Inner Mongolia and an all-out enemy invasion was at hand. (Chiang had received these reports too but had chosen to downplay them.) In return for a united front against the Japanese, Chou said, the Reds would suspend all of their efforts to spread the Communization of China. This would mean an end to the program for seizing landlords' farms and turning them over to the peasants. It would also mean that the Reds would accept Chiang Kai-shek as China's leader and commander-in-chief of all the nation's armies, both those of the Reds and those of the Kuomintang. (Chou En-lai did not say that this would be a temporary arrangement that would end when the enemy was driven from the country, but both he and Chiang were shrewd enough to understand this.)

Chiang at first said very little in response to Chou's skillful presentation. But what little he did say indicated a growing sympathy with the proposal. There can be little doubt, of course, that Chiang saw a united front with the Reds as the best way to end their threat to his regime. Once the Reds were again under Chiang's command and the Japanese were defeated, there would be nothing to prevent Chiang's Kuomintang troops from again turning on Mao's Red troops and destroying them as Chiang had attempted to do earlier at Shanghai and Canton. It was also true, of course, that Mao and Chou had exactly the reverse plan in mind.

Within twenty-four hours word was passed to both the Young Marshal at Sian and Chairman Mao at Paoan that Chiang would agree on a united front with the Reds. There was nothing in writing, but on this verbal agreement Chiang was released, and he and his wife returned to Nanking on Christmas Day, 1936. To prove his good intentions and to attempt an explanation of his purpose in "detaining" Chiang, the Young Marshal flew back with him to Nanking. Chiang returned to a hero's welcome. The airport was crowded with well-wishers, and the streets of Nanking were filled with cheering throngs. Never before—and never afterward—was Chiang Kai-shek so popular with the Chinese people.

Now it was up to Chairman Mao and Chou En-lai to explain the united front to their Red comrades and get them to support it. On this occasion Chairman Mao was aided by the Japanese. Within six months Japan began a mass invasion of China, and all Chinese—Reds, Nationalists, students, warlords, peasants, and factory workers—were forced to forget their differences and fight for their homeland.

The Chinese-Japanese war, which shortly would become just one of the theaters of World War II, began on the night of July 7, 1937, at a place called the Marco Polo Bridge near Peking.

13

Fighting the Japanese

The Marco Polo Bridge incident was wholly manufactured by the Japanese. In the summer of 1937 Japanese troops in Inner Mongolia began to maneuver outside the ancient Chinese city of Peking near the Great Wall. On the night of July 7 a Japanese soldier disappeared from his post while on guard duty at the Marco Polo Bridge. The bridge had been named after the Venetian traveler who had described the stone lions that decorated it. Actually the soldier had deserted his post and was arrested several weeks later by his own command. But by then it was too late.

The Japanese claimed the soldier had been kidnapped by the Chinese and insisted that the kidnapping was an act of war. Generalissimo (or Supreme Commander) Chiang Kai-shek did everything in his power to appease the Japanese, offering to set up an international board of inquiry and making other peace-seeking gestures. But the Japanese would have none of it. Their troops moved into northern Chinese villages, routing out the peasants and claiming they were looking for the kidnapped soldier. When some of these invading troops approached a government arsenal, they were fired upon by Chinese guards, and the war was on.

Almost immediately the Japanese armies poured from Inner Mongolia and Manchuria into northern and northeastern China like a river in flood, sweeping everything before them. By late July Peking and Tientsin had fallen. Shanghai held out a bit longer, but by the end of the year it too fell to the invaders. Shortly afterward the capital city of Nanking was captured. When Nanking fell, Chiang moved his headquarters to Chungking, where it would remain throughout the war.

By the summer of 1938 it seemed that nothing would stop the conquering Japanese. They had, it appeared, defeated Chiang's best armies. They had captured the nation's major industrial centers and taken control of the vital Yangtze River valley. From a military standpoint the Japanese seemed to have won the war, and the outside world expected at any time to learn that Chiang had sued for peace. But the Japanese had not taken into consideration two things: China's vast size, and Mao's Red troops in Shaanxi Province.

During 1938, as the Japanese armies spread across the northern plains and up the Yangtze valley, Generalissimo Chiang, his government, and a major portion of the Chinese population moved west into central and western China.

"You must use space to buy time," Mao urged Chiang, and the Generalissimo adopted this as his policy.

As they moved toward the security of the west, the beleaguered Chinese also adopted a scorched earth policy. They evacuated what they could and destroyed everything else. Fleeing before the Japanese advance, the Chinese took with them not only their food and personal belongings but also industrial machinery and equipment. Whole factories were transported by freight trains, river steamers, frail river junks, and on the backs of coolies to the new western capital of Chungking.

This heroic exodus was similar to the Long March, but on a much vaster scale. It won the sympathy of people outside China. And when reports from neutral observers began to reach the outside world of the atrocities committed by the invading Japanese troops, anger at the Japanese began to mount. When Nanking fell, it was reported, Chinese civilians had been shot, women raped, and private homes looted and destroyed. More than 300,000 civilians had been murdered in a four-week massacre in Nanking after the Chinese government was driven from the city. Hundreds of wounded soldiers who had been left behind in the evacuation were slaughtered, along with their doctors and nurses.

The western world was incensed by these atrocities. Americans had already been angered when the Japanese sank a United States gunboat and three tankers in the Yangtze River near Peking late in 1937. For a few weeks after this incident it appeared that the United States might declare war on Japan. But the government in Tokyo apologized profusely, and President Franklin D. Roosevelt, accurately sensing that the isolationist American public was not yet ready for war, accepted the apology. But after Nanking fell Roosevelt urged that China receive economic and military aid from the United States. Such aid was encouraged by United States businessmen, who had some $250 million invested in China and wanted their investments protected. Since Chiang Kai-shek was a name they were familiar with and one that stood for capitalistic principles, and Mao Tsetung was a virtually unknown anticapitalist Communist, American business interests thought this aid should go directly to Chiang in Chungking.

The first military victories over the conquering Japanese armies during the early months of the war were scored by Mao's Red troops, which under the united front agreement with Chiang had been renamed the Eighth Route Army. Ideally situated in Shaanxi Province, the Eighth Route Army could— and did—successfully attack the Japanese along their west flank as they poured into China.

Generalissimo Chiang urged Mao and his generals, Zhu De and Lin Piao, to use the entire Eighth Route Army in a major attack against the Japanese. But this Mao refused to do. Such a direct confrontation might indeed slow down the Japanese invaders, but it would also probably destroy the Eighth Route Army—a result that Mao suspected Chiang favored as much as he favored defeating the Japanese. Instead Mao ordered Zhu De and Lin Piao once again to employ guerrilla tactics against the enemy. Mao instinctively realized that this was going to be a long war and that the army that held out the longest would win. The Long March had taught him the importance of survival at all costs.

The Eighth Route Army's greatest early victory in the Chinese- or Sino-Japanese War was won on September 26, 1937. A few days earlier Eighth Route Army scouts reported to their headquarters that the Japanese were going to attempt a breakthrough at a place called Pingshin Pass in the loess hills near the Great Wall. Led by Lin Piao, a detachment of Red guerrillas immediately began a forty-eight-hour forced march to intercept the enemy. When the two divisions of Japanese infantry troops arrived at the pass, Lin Piao and his guerrillas were already lying in wait for them. The guerrillas hid in the caves in the hills above the pass until the enemy divisions began to move through the narrow ravine below. Then Lin Piao and his men swarmed down on the unsuspecting Japanese, killing some 6,500 of them at a loss of only 300 Red soldiers.

When word of the victory reached Mao, he was delighted. "So this is the so-called invincible Japanese Imperial Army!" he said. Then he added, "The victory was won with no thanks to the Kuomintang."

Generalissimo Chiang made every effort to downplay the victory, saying Mao's guerrilla efforts were like using straws to stop a tiger. But perhaps challenged by Mao's Eighth Route Army's success, Chiang spurred his Kuomintang forces into an even more sizable victory against the Japanese in Shantung Province several months later. Outside the city of Suchow the Kuomintang intercepted a Japanese force which they outnumbered five to one. In an orthodox, head-on attack the Kuomintang overwhelmed the Japanese, killing more than 10,000 of them and capturing a large number of tanks, armored cars, and weapons. It was significant that this victory was publicized and celebrated throughout China and announced to the western world, while no public notice was paid to the Eighth Route Army's victory. This practice held true virtually throughout the war.

In fighting the Japanese, both the Kuomintang and the Eighth Route Army soldiers found they had encountered a new kind of enemy—a kind not even Chinese army veterans had met before. This enemy was trained in a code called Bushido. It meant, among other things, that no Japanese soldier would allow himself to be taken prisoner if he could possibly avoid doing so. When the Chinese went to the aid of wounded Japanese, the wounded men were apt to jab bayonets into the Chinese who were trying to help them. One Chinese soldier who tried to carry a wounded Japanese soldier on his back had his ear bitten off. Often retreating Japanese troops would booby-trap the wounded they were leaving behind so that a hand grenade would explode when the wounded soldiers were moved. This sort of self-destructive fanaticism—the Japanese soldiers believed it was a disgrace to be taken prisoner—would soon become all too familiar to soldiers fighting the Japanese in World War II.

The Chinese strategy of trading space for time gradually proved successful against the enemy, as Mao knew it must. One of his basic guerrilla rules was "When the enemy attacks, we retreat." Now he knew that at least as far as the Eighth Route Army was concerned, all the other guerrilla tactics must be called into play, especially "When the enemy halts, we harass. When he tires, we attack." Basically this meant making quick, savage, hit-and-run attacks, and infiltrating behind the enemy lines to attack from the rear.

The Japanese high command in Tokyo had worked out a timetable for victory over the Chinese in the Sino-Japanese War. At the end of eighteen months the Chinese were expected to sue for peace. Then Japan could turn its attention to more important enemies—the United States and Great Britain, for example. But when these eighteen months had come and gone, three-quarters of China still remained to be conquered and there was no sign of surrender. The Japanese had sent more than a million men into action, a third of whom had become casualties. With no end to the war in sight, the Japanese began to send out peace signals. Their plan was to concentrate their gains and then return to the attack at a more convenient later date. These peace signals went unheeded by the Chinese, however, and the fighting continued, although on a much reduced scale. The war had, in fact, become a stalemate.

At Eighth Route Army headquarters, which were now in Yenan, Chairman Mao, Chou En-lai, and their generals, along with the Communist Party Central Committee, used this period to consolidate their own position in Shaanxi Province. Under the united front agreement their area was no longer called a soviet. It had been renamed the Northwest Border Region and was considered a political unit of Nationalist China. But in everything but name the Northwest Border Region remained a Communist stronghold and Chairman Mao—technically he was no longer "Chairman" but an officer in Generalissimo Chiang's army, paid a salary of $5 a month by Chiang's government—set about making his organization stronger than ever.

In Yenan Mao also now found time for more personal matters. One of these was divorcing his wife, Ho Tzu-chen, so he could marry a young actress who had recently arrived in Yenan from Shanghai. The young actress's name was Lan Ping, or "Blue Apple," but this was not her original name—nor was it to be her last. Soon she would choose a new name. It would be Jiang Qing, meaning "Green Waters" or "Pure Waters."

When Mao announced his decision to divorce Ho, it caused great consternation in the Communist ranks. Mao was now so well known that any decisions of a personal nature he made had to be approved by the Party. In addition, Ho was a loyal Party member who had borne the Chairman children and had shared with him the trials of the Long March. A meeting of the full Central Committee had to be held to decide the matter.

What influence Mao brought to bear on the Central Committee is not known. What is known is that the Chairman and Ho Tzu-chen were divorced, and shortly afterward Ho left Yenan for the Soviet Union, reportedly for medical treatment of the shrapnel wounds she had suffered during the Long March. In late 1938 or early 1939 Mao married Jiang Qing, who would remain at the Chairman's side for the rest of his life. One of the requirements made by the Central Committee in allowing the divorce and marriage to take place was that Mao's new wife, Jiang Qing, would not be allowed to play any role in public affairs. After all, the Committee reasoned, Ho had been a noble veteran of the Long March and a loyal Party member, while Jiang Qing was just a movie actress who had not "paid her Communist Party dues." Until she had, she must remain a housewife and political nonperson.

There were those among the Central Committee who would one day regret their belittling of Jiang Qing. Meanwhile, she married Mao and silently bided her time.

In Chinese Communist Party history the era between the end of the Long March and the end of World War II is known as the Yenan Period. It is regarded as a milestone along the road to Red success in gaining control of China. During a major part of the Yenan Period, following Mao's marriage and while the stalemate in the Sino-Japanese War continued, the Eighth Route Army gained wider and wider control of the Northwest Border area.

Although Generalissimo Chiang and his Kuomintang troops lay holed up in the mountain fastness in and around Chungking, the Eighth Route Army continued to go into action behind the Japanese lines. The Red Army did not act alone, however. With it went political cadres to preach and teach Communism to the people. Mao had taught his soldiers that a true people's army must move "like fish in water." This meant they must adapt their ways to the environment and never disturb the local peasants' way of life. As the Red guerrillas, in bands of only a thousand or so, drove out the Japanese by constant harassment, the Red political cadres moved in to teach the peasants the Communist practice that everyone from lowliest follower to top leader share and share alike. Communism, they said, would be the Chinese form of government after the war. Then the Communist dictum would become a reality: "To each according to his needs; from each according to his ability."

One of the reasons Mao was so successful in rallying peasants to the Communist cause was the fact that they were disillusioned with Chiang's Nationalists. Ever since they had come into power the Nationalists had promised to help the rural peasants, but no help had ever come. The kind of radical rural reform offered by the Communists—taking the land away from the landlords and dividing it up among the peasants—had an instant appeal to farmers who had worked all their lives in the fields at starvation wages or no wages at all, while the landlords for whom they worked grew rich. "Land to those who till it" was Mao's pledge. The landlords, of course, backed Chiang and the Kuomintang because they promised to protect private property.

Mao also called upon the peasants' patriotism. In rallying them to his side, he urged them first to drive out the Japanese enemy from their homeland. Then, he promised when the homeland was once again theirs, the peasants would have a full and honest share in it. The popular feeling among the peasants against the Kuomintang exploiters and their hatred of the Japanese invaders combined to make the Yenan Period a time of explosive growth in the Communist ranks.

The result of Mao and his colleagues' efforts saw the expansion of the Red Army to more than half a million men by 1940. And Communist Party membership expanded to more than 200,000 by the end of that same year. Also by 1940 more than fifty million Chinese people had elected, by "voting with their feet," to migrate into Mao's Northwest Border Region.

The steady growth of the Communist forces behind the shield of the united front was accurately regarded by Generalissimo Chiang as a major threat to his regime. To end this threat, the Generalissimo stopped sending the Reds any weapons, ammunition, or supplies after 1939. Nor did aid from any outside nation reach any Chinese armies except Chiang's. Again for the Reds the guerrilla rule had to apply: "The enemy supplies our weapons." For Chiang Kai-shek was regarded by the western world—and for that matter by the Soviet Union as well—as the true leader of the Chinese people. Outside China, Mao was regarded as merely a popular rural reformer. Stalin, in fact, stated repeatedly that Mao was not really a Communist.

Chiang, of course, not only accepted all such outside aid in the name of the Chinese governing party, the Nationalists, but he also urged the United States and Great Britain to become his full-fledged allies against Japan. He thought this would happen when World War II began in Europe in September 1939. But he did not get his wish until the Japanese attacked the United States fleet at Pearl Harbor, Hawaii, on December 7, 1941.

14

The Yanks Are Coming

When the United States entered World War II, American flyers had already been fighting the Japanese in China for several months. These were the famed "Flying Tigers," American aerial soldiers of fortune, recruited by a retired United States Army Air Corps officer, Captain Claire L. Chennault.

Captain Chennault had been formally retired in 1937 due to partial deafness as well as personal difficulties with the army high command. Chennault disagreed with the army's proposed methods for the use of its fighter aircraft in combat. Chennault was then forty-seven. Shortly after his retirement Madame Chiang Kai-shek persuaded him to come to China and train the Chinese Air Corps, of which she was the honorary head.

In China Chennault had an opportunity to put into practice his new ideas about aerial combat. He did not believe in fighter pilots fighting as individuals in lone "dogfights" as had been done in World War I. Instead he believed in teamwork, with two planes and their pilots working together as a single unit. As one plane and pilot concentrated on the attack, the other plane and pilot—the "wingman"—flew protective cover. This was not unlike a blocking back in football running interference for the ball carrier. Not only did Chennault successfully train the Chinese in these tactics, but he also flew with his students into combat against the Japanese and was given unofficial credit for personally shooting down some thirty of the enemy.

The enemy at this time consisted mainly of Japanese bomber planes and their fighter escorts making nightly raids on the newly established Chinese Nationalist headquarters at Chungking. Generalissimo Chiang and his wife had been driven into a state of nervous exhaustion by having to spend most of their nights in the air-raid shelters carved out of the rocky fastness beneath the city. Soon the Chennault-trained Chinese Air Corps shot down so many enemy fighters and bombers that the Japanese decided the raids were too costly to continue.

But Chennault knew that his efforts so far were merely stop-gap defensive measures. By 1940, the Japanese controlled all of China's major ports, and the only major land route was the Burma Road, which led from Burma into southern China and up to Chungking. Despite the fact that it was technically neutral, the United States had for many months been sending huge quantities of food and military supplies into China via the Burma Road.

If the Japanese succeeded in capturing the Burma Road, all supplies would be stopped and China would be cut off from the outside world. This would mean China would have to drop out of the war, and the United States would lose a major land base if and when it went to war against Japan.

By early 1941 Chennault was convinced that it was not a matter of whether but when his country would enter the conflict. Having reached this conclusion, Chennault persuaded President Roosevelt and the U.S. State Department to allow him to recruit an American Volunteer Group (AVG) of flyers to protect the Burma Road.

One hundred and fifty of these volunteers from the U.S. Army Air Corps, the Marine Corps, and the Navy arrived in Burma in the fall of 1941. Their planes were 100 old P-40 fighters, on the noses of which they painted tiger sharks' teeth. Only about half of these planes were ever ready for combat at any one time. In addition to their salaries, which ranged from $600 to $750 a month, the pilots were paid $500 by the Chinese government for every Japanese plane they shot down.

The Flying Tigers ran up a truly remarkable score of "kills" against the Japanese. Officially, bonuses were paid on 299 Japanese planes destroyed between December 1941 and July 1942 in the battle for Burma and the defense of the Burma Road. Unofficially, some 1,500 Japanese airmen were shot down during this period, against a loss of less than a dozen Flying Tiger pilots in combat. Eventually the American Volunteer Group was inducted into the U.S. Fourteenth Army Air Corps and Chennault was given a general's stars, but not before the name of the Flying Tigers—a nickname given them by the Chinese—had been written into legend in the skies over Burma.

After the United States entered the war and Brigadier General Chennault and his Flying Tigers were absorbed by the United States Army Air Corps, Chennault came under the control of the new theater commander, U.S. Army Lieutenant

General Joseph W. Stilwell. The word "control," however, could only be used in the technical military sense. Stilwell was a veteran infantry officer who had little respect or time for what he called the "fly-boys." Consequently, he and Chennault clashed constantly over authority and the best military tactics to use against the Japanese. Stilwell favored the use of ground troops "to dig the enemy out of the trenches." When Chennault, who thought air power and air power alone could end the war, pointed out that there *were* no trenches, the two commanders virtually stopped talking with one another.

Stilwell, who was widely known as "Vinegar Joe," also clashed violently, immediately, and through most of the rest of the war with Chiang Kai-shek. This conflict between Stilwell and Chiang was much more important than the conflict between Stilwell and Chennault, because Chiang was now Supreme Military Commander of the China Theater of War, and Stilwell was simply his chief of staff.

When President Roosevelt sent Stilwell to China as Chiang's aide shortly after Pearl Harbor, the President's firm instructions were: "Keep Chiang and China in the war." Roosevelt, like Chennault, realized that China was essential to the Allied cause if the war in the Pacific was to be won.

Upon his arrival in Chungking, General Stilwell found his main job was not merely keeping Chiang in the war but getting him to fight at all. Some of Chiang's troops were in Burma with Chennault and the British fighting the Japanese, but as far as China itself was concerned, the Kuomintang had not fired a shot at the enemy in months. In fact Stilwell soon learned that the only Chinese troops who were trying to drive the Japanese out of China were those in Mao's Eighth Route Army in the northwest. Stilwell learned this from Chou En-lai, who was Mao's liaison officer in Chungking. Chou also made it clear that if Stilwell continued to have trouble rounding up soldiers among the Kuomintang to fight the enemy, all he had to do was ask for volunteers from Mao's forces and he would have all the trained combat troops he needed. But when Stilwell tried to take advantage of this offer, he met with instant opposition from Generalissimo Chiang. Chiang wanted the Reds bottled up in the northwest, and he fought any effort to break the blockade no matter how sorely needed the Eighth Route Army might be. As historian Barbara Tuchman has pointed out, "From first to last Chiang Kai-shek had one purpose: to destroy the Communists and wait for foreign help to defeat the Japanese."

Stilwell was also overwhelmed by the graft, corruption, and primitive army training methods he found in the Nationalist capital at Chungking. High-ranking government officials and army officers were openly engaged in smuggling and black-market operations. Not only food and clothing went to the highest bidder but also key jobs and army promotions as well. Major warlords who had been incorporated into the Kuomintang insisted upon keeping control of their own troops, so that there were numerous little armies within the loose federation of the Kuomintang army. Top Kuomintang officers had little or no control of these warlords.

The treatment of new recruits in the army was brutal. Poor peasant boys were seized by press gangs who were paid so much a head for each new "recruit." These recruits were roped together and brought into training centers, where the barbaric treatment continued. Basic training lasted for only three weeks. Many trainees starved to death or died of disease, and actual military training was virtually nonexistent. On the rare occasions when they were called upon to fight in China, these Kuomintang private soldiers often had to be roped together again to be led into battle. Desertions among both officers and men were high, and bribes of $100 could buy a soldier out of the service.

Stilwell learned that officially there were about three million men under arms in China, but the Chinese Army was strictly a "paper tiger." The average Chinese soldier wore a thin cotton uniform and straw sandals; each night five men slept under one blanket. In addition to his ancient rifle and a small supply of ammunition, each soldier carried two grenades on his belt. In a sock around his neck he carried dried rice, his only food immediately available in the field. He was also supposed to get 25 ounces of rice per day plus some pickled vegetables and salt and pepper while in garrison, but frequently this ration was cut or eliminated. Pay was about $18 a month, from which at least $10 was deducted for food. Two meals a day were eaten from a common pot, and meals were to be eaten in five minutes.

Under these conditions Stilwell was not surprised that starvation and disease alone caused losses of up to 40 percent in Chiang's armies. Official reaction to such losses was one of indifference, the attitude being that the one thing China had in abundance was men.

When Stilwell suggested to Chiang that radical reforms were essential if the Kuomintang was going to become a sound fighting force, he again met with instant rebuff. Consequently, Stilwell noted in his diary that Chiang was "a stubborn, ignorant, prejudiced, conceited despot." Stilwell also took to referring to Chiang—privately of course—as "Peanut," which was what he thought Chiang with his close-shaved head looked like. Chiang shaved his head to hide his graying hair.

In contrast to Chungking, the Communist Northwest Border Region was almost a model of good government. Men, women, and children worked together on equal terms and were rewarded well for their efforts. Youths readily volunteered for the Eighth Route Army and fought well against the Japanese because they felt they had a stake in the future of China. They were eager to drive the enemy from the soil that they themselves would one day till. And when they were not fighting the enemy, Eighth Route Army soldiers joined the peasants in the fields planting crops that were shared by all.

Stilwell himself was greatly impressed with the Communists' achievements both as farmers and as fighting men and women. He could see why Mao's system of land reforms would make his people want to fight for the land. On the other hand, he felt completely out of sympathy with Chiang and his graft-ridden, corrupt army and its do-nothing attitude as it hibernated in Chungking. Stilwell was frank to admit he knew little or nothing about Marxism-Leninism as a political philosophy. He was a practical man and a rough-and-ready infantry soldier. Results were what he sought, and results were what Mao seemed to get while Chiang did not.

During the first two years of World War II, fighting continued to be fierce between the Japanese and the Reds in the Northwest Border Region. And on the part of the Japanese it continued to be barbaric.

In charge of the Japanese armies in this area was General Yasuji Okamura, and he was given a free hand in destroying the Communists. Okamura's response was to set out on a military plan of extermination that outdid any plan ever conceived by Chiang Kai-shek. Under his command Okamura had a million men, and these men he indoctrinated with the "Three Alls" slogan: "Kill all, burn all, destroy all."

Since the Eighth Route Army guerrillas were difficult to distinguish from civilian Chinese villagers, Okamura's army proceeded to slaughter whole villages of people. His men also shot peasants at work in the fields and then dumped salt in the fields so no crops could grow. As historian William Morwood later observed, "The sack of Nanking was daily repeated in miniature everywhere in the land."

Mao himself later said that "the years 1941 and 1942 were the worst years of the entire war." Mao's guerrillas could not protect the entire peasant population. But they tried. Fighting savagely and without letup, they struck the Japanese columns where they were the most vulnerable and caused at least some delay in the Japanese onslaught.

Mao and his soldiers also helped thousands of villagers to dig long tunnels that could be used for storing grain and also as escape routes. "Dig tunnels deep" was Mao's admonition to the populace of the northern China plains. "Store grain everywhere." But these tunnels all too frequently also served as death traps. When the Japanese discovered them, they herded Chinese prisoners—men, women, and children—into them and then gassed the prisoners to death. Historian Morwood has further stated, "It has been estimated that the population of the rich northern plain decreased from 44 to 25 million during General Okamura's reign of terror."

This extermination campaign lasted until 1943, when General Okamura's army was withdrawn by the Japanese for use elsewhere in the struggle against the United States and Great Britain—a struggle that by then had begun to go against the Japanese. Mao Tsetung and those of his Central Committee comrades who had survived then set about rebuilding the economy and industry of the entire northern area of China.

In a way Okamura had done the Communists a brutal but nonetheless real favor. With no governmental authority except the Communists, who had done their best to defend them against the Japanese, the whole populace of this vast region now turned to Mao and his colleagues and accepted them as their leaders. The Long March had been the ordeal by fire that had tested the mettle of the Communist Party. Now the people of northern China had experienced a similar ordeal at the hands of the Japanese. The survivors of the Long March and the survivors of the Japanese reign of terror now faced the future together. And shrewd political leader that he was, Mao Tsetung did everything in his power to make this bond unseverable. For Mao knew that the final ordeal of the Chinese revolution still lay ahead. It would occur when the war ended and the Communists and the Nationalists faced each other in the final struggle for control of the nation.

Meanwhile, General Stilwell had been undergoing his own ordeal in the crucible of Burma. Before the war Burma had been a British Crown Colony, and when the Japanese had threatened to overrun it shortly after Pearl Harbor, the British had called upon the Chinese for help. It was in China's self-interest to protect the Burma Road, so Generalissimo Chiang Kai-shek had sent two of his armies to Burma in response to the British plea. When Stilwell arrived in Chungking and began to present Chiang with plans for reorganizing the Kuomintang army, Chiang hit on the ingenious and devious idea of ridding himself of Stilwell and yet retaining United States support by offering Stilwell command of the Chinese forces in Burma. Flattered, and innocent about Chiang's motives,

Stilwell eagerly accepted the Generalissimo's offer. It was not one of Vinegar Joe's wisest career decisions.

When Stilwell arrived in Burma, he discovered to his dismay that he was commander of the Chinese forces there in name only. After he presented himself to the local British commander, the British officer expressed surprise to the local Chinese general that the Chinese would accept an inexperienced American officer as their leader when they had refused to accept an experienced British officer in a similar role. The Chinese general replied that Stilwell was not really in command of any Chinese troops. He had just been told he was, to keep him and his superiors happy.

Stilwell also found that the Chinese officers listened to his orders and then blithely ignored them. Part of this was due to the traditional reluctance of the Chinese to say no, but most was due to a stolid refusal to accept orders from an outsider and especially from a white American. Knowing his career was on the line, Stilwell brought all of his leadership abilities—and they were considerable, despite his normally vinegary nature—into play and eventually won the Chinese officers to his side.

For one thing, Stilwell was a fighting man. He did not say, "You go ahead, and I'll follow," in combat situations. He led the way into the most vicious of firefights. Secondly, Stilwell gradually came to have a genuine respect for the Chinese fighting men, and this respect shone through his crusty exterior. He did not respect the Chinese military men in Chungking, where the only combat they waged was in the black market, but he did come to respect the Chinese officers and soldiers fighting in the Burma jungles under the worst possible conditions.

Stilwell had been leading American infantry soldiers all his life, and in one major way he found that the average Chinese infantryman was no different from the average American G.I. If you treated him decently and gave him good rations, equipment, and training, he was on the way to becoming a soldier. Then if you made him understand clearly what needed to be done and how to do it, he would die trying to follow orders. And thousands of Chinese soldiers were to die trying in Burma—mostly to no immediate effect.

The Americans, British, and Chinese were faced with almost impossible odds in Burma. Frequently outnumbered by as much as five to one, they also faced a suicidal foe who was determined to capture the Burma Road and thus cut off China from aid from the outside world. The Allies did their best to stem the tide of onrushing Japanese. Finally, despite heroic efforts, Stilwell and his Chinese were trapped in southern Burma in the spring of 1942.

General Chennault sent a message offering to fly Stilwell out of this trap—leaving behind everyone else, of course. But Stilwell turned him down. "The fly-boys didn't get me in here," Vinegar Joe replied from the heart of the Burmese jungles, "and they won't get me out. I'll walk."

Whereupon Stilwell and what was left of his command— some 9,000 men—started the trek toward India. This forced march was made through roadless jungle, across flooded rivers, up and down steep mountains. When word that he had arrived at Imphal, India, on May 20, 1942, was flashed to the outside world, the effort was widely hailed as an epic of courage in the face of enormous odds and compared with Mao's Long March.

But Vinegar Joe left no doubt in anybody's mind that it

was a retreat, not a victory. At a press conference he declared flatly, "I claim we took a hell of a beating. I think we ought to find out what caused it, and then go back and retake it."

What Stilwell began to do next was to train the Chinese under his command in India in American infantry methods. He also got—by demanding them—more men from Chungking and added these trainees to his growing army of skilled combat soldiers. In addition he requested and received equipment and supplies from the United States for this fighting force, with which he had every intention of whipping the Japanese when the Burma campaign was renewed.

In Chungking, Generalissimo Chiang reluctantly allowed these reinforcements—eventually numbering some 45,000 men—to be sent to Stilwell in India. In return, however, Chiang demanded that the United States somehow manage to continue to get supplies into China. Behind Chiang's demands was always the hidden threat that if he did not get his way, China would drop out of the war.

Another epic feat was necessary to meet Chiang's demands. It was performed by the United States Army Air Forces. Even before the Burma Road was cut off it had been decided to use C-47 cargo planes to ferry supplies from India to China, crossing the high Himalaya mountains at altitudes up to 20,000 feet. At first this plan to fly over "the Hump" seemed impossible. The two-engine, propeller-driven—there were no jet-powered aircraft in those days—transport planes did not have pressurized cabins, so the crews would have to use oxygen tanks and masks much of the way. And the slow-flying transports would be able to do little to defend themselves against Japanese fighter plane attacks.

But many airmen volunteered to risk their lives in the effort.

In April 1942 ten C-47s flew over the Hump, ferrying into China a first historic cargo: 30,000 gallons of precious aviation gasoline. With the use of larger planes such as the four-engine C-54s, the airlift tonnage gradually increased until it reached a total of 71,000 tons a month by the end of the war—far more than had been delivered over the Burma Road. This effort was not without cost in men and equipment. During the course of the war, 850 American airmen were killed and 250 planes were destroyed flying over the Hump. But their sacrifice helped keep China in the war.

Stilwell was convinced that in addition to the airlift of supplies into China, another ground route must be provided. Consequently, with American-trained Chinese combat troops leading the way, U.S. Army Engineers began to blast a new mountain road from Ledo in India to northern Burma. When the Ledo (later Stilwell) Road was finished, it would link up with a section of the old Burma Road in northern Burma that had not been cut by the Japanese and would then lead directly into southern China. Thousands of Chinese coolies were also pressed into service to complete the Ledo-Stilwell Road, and their superhuman task was not unlike that of their ancestors who had built China's Great Wall.

Stilwell's forces were not able to resume their campaign directly against the Japanese in Burma until late in the war. Building the Ledo-Stilwell Road and fighting off attacks by the Japanese on his headquarters at Imphal prevented Stilwell from mounting counterattacks of his own. In addition, the Japanese began a massive campaign to knock out the American airfields that Chennault had set up along the Chinese coast.

When the attack on the American airfields began, Stilwell flew to Chungking and again tried to goad Generalissimo

Chiang into action against the Japanese. When Chiang continued to be reluctant to move, Stilwell demanded that he put
him in complete command of the Nationalist forces. This
Chiang flatly refused to do. Chiang also asked the United States
to recall Stilwell from China.

Vinegar Joe was replaced as Chiang's aide by Major General
Albert C. Wedemeyer in October 1944. Wedemeyer was a
great admirer of Chiang and sympathetic to the Nationalist
cause. But the American general was not in the country long
before he too realized that, as far as Chiang was concerned,
the war in China was as much a fight against the Chinese
Communists as against the Japanese. For some months now
the so-called alliance of the Kuomintang and Mao's Eighth
Route Army had been broken, and Chiang was once again
attempting to exterminate the Communists.

In the spring and early summer of 1945 Wedemeyer and
various other American advisers finally convinced Chiang that
he should stop killing Communists and mount an offensive
against the Japanese. By this time Japan was suffering severe
reverses throughout the Pacific Theater of War, and as soon
as the Nationalists began to fight them in China, the Japanese
gave up their earlier Chinese conquests. In Burma the Japanese
also retreated steadily before renewed attacks by the British
and Stilwell's former forces from India. The Stilwell Road
was now complete, and soon the whole of Burma was liberated.
The war in Europe had ended with the surrender of Germany
on May 7. On August 6 and 9, 1945, the United States dropped
atomic bombs on the Japanese cities of Hiroshima and Naga-
saki. Soon afterward the Japanese surrendered.

During the course of World War II, China—or the China,
Burma, India (CBI) theater—was never regarded by most ob-

servers as anything more than a sideshow in the main Pacific Theater of War. But now the China sideshow was about to become the main act. Soon the Communist revolutionaries led by Mao's newly named People's Liberation Army would sweep Chiang and his Kuomintang out of China and onto the island of Formosa (Taiwan) in the neighboring sea. In this drama the United States would play a major role.

15

America Backs the Wrong Horse

When he returned to the United States near the end of World War II, General Stilwell maintained a public silence regarding the situation in China. But in a private conversation with Secretary of War Henry L. Stimson, Stilwell said flatly, "Nothing can be done in China until we get rid of Chiang Kai-shek." At the end of the war, shortly before his death from cancer on October 12, 1946, Stilwell made it clear that he thought "the United States should get out of China—*now*."

Stilwell's conviction that the United States should get out of China was based on his certain knowledge that, when World War II ended, there would be a Chinese civil war between Chiang's Kuomintang and Mao's Red Army. Stilwell was also convinced that the Communist forces would win this war. He thought that if the United States ended its support of Chiang and backed Mao and the Communists—or "agricultural liberals," as Stilwell called them—there might be established a sound base on which to build future U.S.–China relations. Otherwise the United States would find itself in a "no-win" situation.

But Stilwell was realistic enough to know that the United States would never back the Communists. Most Americans were convinced that the Communists were out to conquer the world. Russian Communists and Chinese Communists, they thought, were all alike: a Communist was a Communist. Stilwell did not agree with this assessment, but he knew it would be political suicide for any American president or other elected official to suggest dropping Chiang in favor of Mao. General Stilwell died convinced that the United States would continue to "back the wrong horse."

And he was right.

More than six months before the end of World War II, Mao Tsetung and Chou En-lai made a formal request through General Wedemeyer's headquarters in China that they be allowed to come to Washington to talk with President Roosevelt. The purpose of this proposed visit was to present the Reds' side of the political situation in China and to try to develop a working relationship with the United States that did not favor the Kuomintang exclusively. In other words, Mao and Chou were seeking cooperation and friendship with the United States.

Mao and Chou's request was completely ignored.

Despite this rebuff, the Reds went along with U.S. Ambassador Patrick J. Hurley's attempts to work out plans for a future coalition government between the Communists and the Kuomintang. When this plan was presented to Chiang Kai-shek, however, the Generalissimo flatly rejected it as a threat by the Communists to take over the entire Chinese government. Letting the Communists take part in the Chinese government, Chiang said, would be like putting a fox in the henhouse.

Mao Tsetung then turned to U.S. State Department officers who had been sent to Mao's headquarters at Yenan to act as observers. He tried to convince them that he and his followers would one day head the Chinese government even if it took a civil war to put them in power. At least two of these foreign service political officers, John S. Service and John P. Davies, were convinced that ignoring Mao and supporting only Chiang would not unify postwar China. Davies, in fact, went so far as to say in one report to Washington that the Communists had "positive and widespread popular support. China's destiny is not Chiang's but theirs."

On April 25, 1945, with victory in World War II in sight, President Franklin D. Roosevelt died. He was succeeded in office by his Vice President, Harry S. Truman. When the war ended, Truman tried to carry out Roosevelt's postwar plans, including the firm establishment of China as a major power in the Pacific. Like Roosevelt, Truman saw Chiang Kai-shek as the only man strong enough to rule a powerful postwar China. But first China must be unified. Truman encouraged Ambassador Hurley to continue his unification efforts, all of which ended in failure.

Finally, on November 25, 1945, the frustrated Hurley resigned as Ambassador, charging that "a considerable section of our State Department is endeavoring to support Communism generally as well as specifically in China." These charges caused a sensation in the United States. Several members of the State Department were recalled from China, and their careers were eventually ruined. Service and Davies were, in fact, dismissed from the foreign service.

Attempting to salvage something from this tragic fiasco in foreign affairs, Truman appointed General George C. Marshall as a special ambassador to try to unite China. Chief of Staff during World War II, Marshall had just retired, and he would soon become Truman's Secretary of State. But Marshall's mission also ended in failure.

Marshall, however, did succeed in prevailing upon Mao Tse-tung, Chou En-lai, and their aides to confer with Chiang Kai-shek first at Chungking and then at Nanking, which was once again the Nationalist capital. Mao was immediately suspicious of how agreeable Chiang was regarding Marshall's suggestions for a coalition between the Communists and the Kuomintang. Mao's suspicions were confirmed when he learned that Chiang was using the conferences as cover-ups for getting Kuomintang forces into position to drive the Reds out of northern China. Shortly after this discovery the final meeting broke up, and Mao and his aides returned to Yenan to prepare for all-out civil war.

Before he left for the United States, Marshall, as frustrated now as Hurley had been, held a final meeting with Chiang. Marshall told Chiang that he must get his house in order by ridding his government of graft and corruption or he never could succeed in getting the support of the Chinese people. Marshall also implied that a thorough housecleaning was necessary if Chiang wanted continued United States support. Chiang assured Marshall that he was already readying a new broom to begin a clean sweep within his government household. But first things must come first, he added. All of Marshall's suggested reforms would be taken care of just as soon as the

Communists were defeated. This was a siren song that Marshall and other Americans before him had heard many times, but once again it had an appealing sound. Marshall asked Chiang how long he thought that would take. "Less than a year," Chiang said, "with continued U.S. aid."

Military man Marshall was interested in just how Chiang proposed to wage his final campaign against the Reds. The present situation, Chiang explained, was quite similar to the situation in 1934 when the Kuomintang had surrounded the Communists in southern China during Chiang's Fifth Annihilation Campaign. Now he had the Communists surrounded in Shaanxi Province in northern China. This time, however, the Kuomintang—thanks to the United States—had modern airplanes and tanks at its disposal. The Red bandits would not be able to break out again and start another Long March. There would, in fact, be no place to go on a Long March, or a short march either for that matter. *This* time his extermination campaign would be totally successful.

The all-out civil war between the Kuomintang and the People's Liberation Army began in the spring of 1946. Most of the early fighting was not in Shaanxi Province, as Chiang had predicted, but in Manchuria, which had been evacuated by the defeated Japanese and then occupied by the Soviet Union near the end of World War II. When the Russians moved out of Manchuria as part of the peace agreement, they left behind weapons, ammunition, and military equipment they had captured from the Japanese. This World War II materiel was seized by Mao's forces. But the Russians took with them all the heavy equipment and tools needed to operate the rich mines in Manchuria, a move for which the Chinese never forgave them.

When the civil war began, the People's Liberation Army also captured many additional weapons and much ammunition in their first battles with the Kuomintang. These battles were won with relative ease by the seasoned Red troops against the poorly trained and inexperienced Nationalists. Most important of all, however, was the fact that tens of thousands of Nationalist troops soon began to desert the Kuomintang and join the People's Liberation Army. Chairman Mao commented on this situation by saying, "Chiang Kai-shek is both our best supply sergeant and our best recruiting officer." By the end of the civil war almost a million Nationalist soldiers had joined the Reds. Many of these defectors later fought against the Americans in Korea.

When Chiang Kai-shek realized that he could no longer keep the Communist forces bottled up in northern China, he became desperate. His requests for additional aid in money and military equipment from the United States doubled. At first these requests were honored by the United States, and Chiang was able to mount a major offensive against the Communist headquarters and seat of government at Yenan.

When the offensive against Yenan began, Mao countered by simply moving his headquarters and its 250,000-man defensive garrison out of the city. This maneuver, Mao reasoned, would satisfy Chiang's desire to capture cities while it would not harm the Communists in the least. "Let him have the empty city," Mao said.

Despite the fact that the Nationalists had captured nothing but empty urban real estate in taking Yenan, newspapers around the world and especially in the United States heralded the event as a great victory for Chiang and predicted an early end to the war. One newspaper headline read: "CHINESE NA-

TIONALISTS CAPTURE RED STRONGHOLD." What was not headlined was that by 1947 the Chinese People's Liberation Army controlled most of the countryside throughout northern China, and the fact that the Nationalists held several key cities was relatively meaningless. This situation was to be echoed some years later in the Vietnam War, when American generals kept announcing that they controlled the major cities in South Vietnam, but failed to disclose that the enemy, the Vietcong, controlled the countryside.

In China control of the cities and a failure to control the countryside often resulted in bitter comedy. A trainload of Nationalist troops would start out from a city only to find when they reached the city's outskirts that Red guerrillas had removed all the railroad tracks.

By 1948 Mao was able to offer Chiang something else he had long sought—an end to guerrilla warfare and a major battle between the Nationalist and the Communists. This battle took place in Shantung Province, and when it was over Chiang's reign on the Chinese mainland was nearing its end.

After gaining control of Manchuria, Mao's next major goal was Peking, which he intended to make the capital of Communist China. When Peking did not immediately fall, the Communist forces simply put it and the neighboring port city of Tientsin under siege and marched on around them toward the south and Nanking.

At this point Chiang became truly desperate, for if the Nationalist capital fell, the war would clearly be lost. He sent his wife to Washington to plead with President Truman and the U.S. Congress for additional funds as well as for American officers to lead Chinese troops in the coming battle for Nationalist China.

Back during World War II Madame Chiang had made a similar fund-raising trip to the United States that had turned into something of a triumphal tour. She had spoken before a joint session of the Congress, stayed in the White House, and then gone on a speaking tour of U.S. cities to rally Americans to the Chinese cause—actually that of Generalissimo Chiang. A woman of vast charm, Madame Chiang had been acclaimed everywhere, and funds had poured in. That propaganda effort had been an enormous success.

But this time she did not arrive—or leave—in triumph. President Truman and many other U.S. politicians had become more than a little disenchanted with Chiang. They had begun to see him as an inept and bungling general, and reports from Generals Wedemeyer and Marshall and others had made it clear that Chiang's government was hopelessly corrupt.

This time Madame Chiang wanted $3 billion in military aid. Two and a half billion dollars had already gone to aid Chiang's postwar efforts in China, and Truman was not about to offer any more. He told his aides: "I'll bet you a billion dollars of that first two and a half billion is in Chiang's Swiss bank account right now."

There were, of course, many Chinese Nationalist and Chiang sympathizers in Washington. This group, which was also violently opposed to Communists and Communism in any form, was known as the China Lobby. The China Lobby thought the world as they knew it would come to an end if Mao came to power in China, so its members rallied to Madame Chiang's support. In the end, however, Madame Chiang had to return to China virtually empty-handed.

Meanwhile, Generalissimo Chiang began to prepare a text-book defense of Nanking. The Yangtze River, on which Nanking is situated, had always formed a natural barrier to invading armies from the north. Chiang, however, decided he would stop the People's Liberation Army before it reached the Yangtze. To do this he established his main battle line along the Hwai River 100 miles (160 km) to the north of Nanking.

Chiang had more than half a million troops at his disposal, including several divisions trained by General Stilwell. These troops were stationed along a 50-mile (80-km) front from Suchow to the coastal town of Haichow at the mouth of the Hwai. Because of where it was fought, this classic conflict became known as the Battle of Hwai-Hai ("Hwai" for the river and "Hai" for the port of Haichow).

Mao's forces outnumbered Chiang's by roughly fifty thousand men, including one army led by the formidable General Lin Biao, who was known as the One-Eyed Dragon. Lin had been shot in the eye during the Long March but had recovered from this severe wound and gone on to become something of a folk hero in Red battles against the Japanese. General Lin Biao was to be in charge of one corps of the People's Liberation Army in the coming battle, and the second corps would be commanded by General Lin Piao, another Long March hero. The two Lins were sometimes known as "Thunder and Lightning," with Lin Biao delivering thunderous hammer blows against the enemy and Lin Piao striking like lightning.

While Mao and Chou En-lai and their political comrades were conferring with their generals before the battle, a telegram was delivered at Red headquarters. The telegram was from Joseph Stalin. In it Stalin urged Mao not to defeat the Kuomintang too quickly or too decisively. As historian Morwood and others have pointed out, the telegram implied that an overwhelming defeat of the Nationalists by the People's Liberation

Army might start all the Western nations on a worldwide military crusade against Communism. The Soviet Union was already engaged in a Cold War with the United States and other Western powers, and Stalin did not want it to become a hot one. After Russia's enormous losses in World War II, the Soviet Union could ill afford another conflict.

Mao was well aware of the bitter irony of the Stalin message. After years of ignoring the Chinese Reds and calling them "Radish Communists"—red on the outside and white on the inside—Stalin was suddenly aware that Mao and his People's Liberation Army were truly a force to reckon with. But the telegram also made it clear that Stalin was still at least half convinced that Chiang was the only leader who could control the Chinese people. Stalin's telegram was not answered.

Mao expected the Hwai-Hai battle to last for the last two months of 1948 and perhaps well into 1949. But almost immediately the fighting went in favor of the Reds. Striking thunder-and-lightning blows at the center of the Kuomintang battle line, the corps of the two Lins divided the enemy into two separate forces. The Reds then encircled the divided forces and began to squeeze them into smaller and smaller isolated positions. Then, guerrillalike, the Red corps harried the defenders on the outer rims of these circles.

Within a matter of days, Chiang's Kuomintang divisions began to desert to the Communists. From Nanking, Chiang directed that reinforcements be sent by sea to his beleaguered troops. But the Reds had occupied the coast and prevented the reinforcements from landing. Chiang then ordered numerous American-made tanks to relieve the surrounded Kuomintang. But the Reds had dug tank traps to prevent just such a maneuver, and the tanks floundered to a halt.

Although the battle—the largest in Chinese history—went on for several more weeks, its outcome was never seriously in doubt. More and more of the Kuomintang defected to the Communists, and by the turn of the year, when the battle ended, Chiang's forces had dwindled to only a third of their original size. This third, however, including a division led by graduates of the Whampoa Military Academy, fought on valiantly. Knowing that the battle was lost, Chiang ordered his own positions bombarded to prevent Kuomintang military equipment and supplies from falling into the hands of the Reds.

Early in 1949 Peking and Tientsin surrendered, and almost all of north China was in Communist hands. Faced with the total collapse of his armies and the imminent fall of Nanking, Chiang Kai-shek resigned as President of the Republic of China. His successors offered to negotiate peace terms, and brief peace talks were held in Peking. But these peace talks broke down in April when it became clear that the Nationalists had little to offer and the Communists demanded what amounted to unconditional surrender.

A few days later the Communists moved into Nanking, and by the end of May they had occupied Shanghai. Although much of southern China still remained to be conquered by the People's Liberation Army, Mao knew it was just a matter of time until this final phase was completed. On October 1, 1949, as his armies continued their last campaigns of the civil war, Chairman Mao held a triumphal ceremony in Peking. At this ceremony he proclaimed the establishment of the new Chinese Communist state: the People's Republic of China.

Generalissimo Chiang Kai-shek remained in south and southwest China until December 10, 1949. Then, following the hundreds of thousands of Nationalist Chinese refugees who had already fled from the Reds to the neighboring island of Formosa (Taiwan), Chiang also sought safety on that island. Chiang had had the foresight to send ahead to Taiwan a vast hoard of gold, the Nationalist government's treasury reserve, so he was financially able to maintain a government in exile, as well as to maintain himself and his wife and their aides in the manner to which they had long been accustomed. The Nationalist loyalists in the United States as well as the United States government itself also helped Chiang replenish his war chest with money as well as war materiel against the day when, as Chiang vowed, he and his armies would retake the mainland. Meanwhile, on March 1, 1950, Chiang again took the title of President of the Republic of China, which his successors and their allies both at home and abroad still claim is the only true and free China.

The vast mainland of China, however, still was occupied by upward of a billion people—a quarter of the world's population. It was now up to Chairman Mao to establish a new government over this great landmass and its myriad peoples, as he had so long dreamed of doing. The Long March to gain control of China had ended. But the equally long and in many ways even more difficult march to govern the Chinese nation had just begun.

16

Brief Alliance
With the Soviet Union

Heading the new People's Republic of China was, of course, Chairman Mao Tsetung. Vice Chairman was Liu Shao-chi. Chou En-lai became Premier and was put in control of all government departments and ministries.

The naming of Liu Shao-chi as second in command was something of a surprise, but it was a clear indication of Chairman Mao's plans for the immediate future. Liu was not a veteran of the Long March, but he was a long-time Communist Party member and organizer. Most significant of all, however, was the fact that he had studied in Moscow and had maintained close ties with the Soviet Union since his youth.

Mao knew that he was going to need massive financial help to rebuild China. When it became clear that the United States and many other Western nations were going to continue to recognize the Nationalists on Taiwan as the only legal government of China, Mao accepted the fact that his People's Republic must turn elsewhere for foreign aid. Realist that he was, Mao also knew that the country to which he must turn was the Soviet Union. Vice Chairman Liu would be an ideal ambassador to arrange talks between Mao and Russian Premier Stalin.

Such talks were arranged, and in December of 1949 Chairman Mao journeyed to Moscow. This was the fifty-six-year-old Mao's first trip outside China.

Stalin too was a supremely pragmatic person, and if he once had had doubts about Mao's becoming the leader of Communist China, he could have few doubts now. Stalin quickly agreed to loan China the equivalent of sixty million dollars annually for five years. The loan was to be used in setting up fifty large state-owned factories that would be the backbone of the new China's modern industry. During the two months Mao spent in Russia, he also signed a Treaty of Friendship and Mutual Assistance with the Soviet Union.

When Mao returned to China, he immediately turned his attention to the problem of rural land reform. This problem had become more and more pressing as the People's Liberation Army cleared out the last remaining Kuomintang forces from southern and southwestern China. As the Kuomintang was driven out of vast rural areas, the oppressed peasants began taking matters into their own hands. Many rich landlords were killed and their lands taken over by the peasants. While Mao and his government had promised the widespread redistribution of all farmlands, it was important to do so in an orderly fashion in order to quickly restore agricultural production. Otherwise the new China might face a famine.

In June 1950, while Mao and his government were in the midst of reorganizing the nation's economy, a new war began—this time in neighboring Korea.

When it declared war on Japan near the end of World War II, the Soviet Union occupied not only Manchuria but also Korea. At the end of the war it was agreed that Russia would accept the surrender of Japanese troops north of the 38th parallel of latitude in Korea and the United States would accept the surrender of Japanese troops south of the 38th parallel. This effectively divided Korea into two separate governments, North and South Korea.

The Koreans, who had long sought complete independence, were dissatisfied with this arrangement. They wanted to hold elections to unify their country. They were backed in this demand by the newly formed world peacekeeping organization, the United Nations. No such elections were allowed in Soviet-controlled North Korea. They were, however, held in South Korea, where Syngman Rhee was elected President of the new and independent Republic of Korea.

Soon afterward both Soviet and United States military forces began to withdraw from divided Korea. Skirmishes between North and South Korean forces continued along the 38th parallel for many months. Then, in the early morning of June 25, 1950, the Soviet-equipped military forces of Communist North Korea invaded South Korea. Their mission was to unite the country by force.

At this juncture the last thing that Red China needed was to become involved in yet another war. The economic reconstruction of war-torn China had barely begun, and Mao and his government desperately needed a long period of peace to restore their country's agriculture and industry. Nevertheless,

Mao immediately indicated Red China's readiness to aid Communist North Korea in the new conflict. Chinese soldiers began fighting in Korea in October 1950 and fought there until the war's end almost three years later.

The United States, backed by the United Nations, immediately reinforced South Korea, and soon a full-scale war was under way on the Korean peninsula. As part of this war effort, President Truman ordered the United States Seventh Fleet to patrol the waters of the Strait of Taiwan between mainland China and the new Nationalist stronghold on Taiwan. This was done, Truman said, to prevent Red China from capturing Taiwan and posing a greater threat to the Free World.

Mao was quick to denounce Truman's "neutralization" of the offshore China waters and intervention in Korea as "open acts of imperialism." In an accusation that would apply not only to the Korean War but also later to the Vietnam War, Mao declared on June 28, 1950: "The Chinese people have long since affirmed that the affairs of the various countries throughout the world should be run by the peoples of those countries, and that the affairs of Asia should be run by the peoples of Asia and not by the United States. U.S. aggression in Asia will only arouse widespread and resolute resistance by the peoples of Asia. Truman stated on 5 January this year that the United States would not interfere in Taiwan. Now he has proved his own statement to be false, and has torn to shreds all the international agreements regarding noninterference by the United States in the internal affairs of China. The United States has thus exposed its own imperialist face and this is beneficial to the people of China and of all Asia. There is no reason at all for U.S. intervention in the internal affairs of Korea, the Philippines, Vietnam, or other countries. The sympathy of the people throughout China, as well as the broad masses of the people everywhere in the world, is on the side of the victims of aggression, and most decidedly not on the side of U.S. imperialism."

Earlier, General Stilwell had accurately predicted that the United States would wind up in a no-win situation if it continued to try to control the internal politics of China—an effort that historian Henry Steele Commager has called "certainly the greatest blunder in the history of American diplomacy." In the Korean War the United States also wound up in a no-win situation. The conflict eventually became a stalemate, with neither side able to claim victory. Although a truce agreement was signed on July 27, 1953, at Panmunjom, Korea, no final peace agreement was ever reached. Peace talks continue to this day, and Korea remains a divided nation.

Whether or not the United States and the United Nations accomplished their purpose in the Korean War is still a matter of speculation among historians. An equally interesting speculation is what would have happened if the United States had earlier recognized Chairman Mao's People's Republic of China rather than Chiang Kai-shek's discredited Nationalist regime. If this course had been followed by the United States, it is highly doubtful that there would ever have been a Korean War—or, for that matter, a Vietnam War.

Immediately after the Korean War the People's Republic of China renewed its all-out efforts at economic reform and recovery on the Chinese mainland. A Soviet-style Five Year Plan was begun to increase farm production and industrial output. Farms and factories were taken over by the government and turned into state-controlled enterprises. The nation's railroad system also was nationalized as well as the school system and all communications media.

Great economic gains began to be made almost at once. Industry expanded by 50 percent during the five-year period, and steel production increased by more than 300 percent. Agriculture also showed significant advances as 500 million peasants on 52,000 sprawling collective farms or communes learned how to work together rather than independently. "Eating out of one big pot," this was called.

Despite these obvious successes, Chairman Mao received few congratulations on a second trip to the Soviet Union. From his cool reception Mao realized that Russian leaders continued to regard China as a third-rate nation. He was treated like the visiting head of a minor Soviet satellite country rather than the head of a major independent power. Mao returned to China with many of his old misgivings about the Soviet Union renewed.

In 1956 Nikita Khrushchev, who had taken over as Premier of the Soviet Union following Stalin's death in 1953, surprised the world by denouncing Stalin and starting a de-Stalinization campaign in Russia. Although there had never been any love lost between Mao and Stalin, Mao did not approve of Khrushchev's denunciation of the dead Russian leader. Mao thought it was disloyal and weakened Chinese as well as Russian Communism. When Khrushchev announced a new Soviet policy of "peaceful coexistence" with the West, Mao angrily charged Khrushchev with turning his back on China.

In 1957 Mao began what he called his "Hundred Flowers Campaign" in China. This was aimed at eliminating all secret-police methods throughout China, methods that had been

encouraged by Mao's Soviet advisers. The campaign also encouraged critics within the Chinese Communist Party to speak out against any Party policies with which they disagreed. This part of the campaign was expressed in the phrase "Let a hundred schools of thought contend."

Now for the first time there began to be sharp disagreement among the Chinese Communist Party leaders. Vice Chairman Liu Shao-chi and his followers opposed any drift away from the arms of "Mother Russia." They also opposed any open debate within the Party regarding government policy. Communist doctrine could not be criticized, they insisted, because whatever Party leaders decided was right. The Liu faction was powerful enough to end Mao's Hundred Flowers Campaign virtually before it had begun.

Mao responded by launching another Five Year Plan for Chinese progress in 1958. This plan was called "The Great Leap Forward." It called for industrial production, especially the production of steel, to be doubled. It also promised to double grain food production within a year.

To meet the Great Leap Forward's steel-production goals, thousands of small furnaces were built to make pig iron. Many of these small furnaces were in the backyards of family dwellings, and there was one on the grounds of Peking National University, where Mao had once worked as an assistant librarian. Pig-iron production soared, but its quality was so poor that the project had to be abandoned. Agriculture showed some improvement during the first year, but then there were crop failures for the next three years, and the country faced a near famine. By 1962 Mao had to admit that the Great Leap Forward had failed. His critics called it the Great Leap Backward.

This failure strengthened the hand of Vice Chairman Liu and his Liu-ist followers in their growing opposition to Mao. But Mao had strengthened his own hand by putting his old Long March comrade, Lin Piao, in charge of the army as Minister of Defense. During the 1960s Lin Piao prepared the army for a lightning stroke against the Liu-ists if they threatened to depose Mao.

It was also during the 1960s that two events took place in the People's Republic of China that startled the Western World. Red China and the Soviet Union severed their alliance, and Chairman Mao's scientists and technicians exploded Communist China's first atomic bomb.

Khrushchev had long made it clear that he and the Soviet Politburo did not favor either Mao's Hundred Flowers Campaign or the Great Leap Forward. The first Khrushchev said he did not even understand, and the second was anti-Communist because Communism did not move forward in leaps and bounds but with relentless steadiness. Khrushchev, like Stalin before him, also objected to the fact that China's Communist government was supported mainly by the rural peasants. It did not have a firm base among city industrial workers, nor did Mao show he sought such a base.

In July 1960 Khrushchev ordered all Soviet technicians working on Chinese industrial projects to return to the Soviet Union. Chairman Mao's response amounted to "Good-bye and good riddance." As far as Mao was concerned, that Khrushchev said a thing was good for Russia did not mean that the same thing was good for China. Mao then set about counterattacking the opposition of Liu and the other dissidents within his own Party by launching the Great Cultural Revolution.

China exploded its first atomic bomb in October 1964. While

Mao gave no indication of planning to use the bomb for foreign aggression, the fact that Red China was now a member—if an unwanted one—of the exclusive nuclear club gave serious pause to the Western powers. This was precisely what Chairman Mao wanted. One way or another Mao was determined to have the People's Republic of China recognized as an important and independent member of the world community of nations.

The Great Cultural Revolution was an expression of Chairman Mao's belief that in order to remain strong the People's Republic of China must continue its revolution. Too many Chinese Communists, especially Communist leaders, had become interested in their own security and prosperity. These self-seeking bureaucrats must not only be named and criticized by the public but must also be driven from office. Foremost among those who must be driven from office were, of course, Vice Chairman Liu Shao-chi and his followers.

On his side in the Cultural Revolution Mao had Premier Chou En-lai, Defense Minister Lin Piao, and Madame Mao—Jiang Qing. Beginning in 1966 and lasting up to the eve of Mao's death in 1976 the Cultural Revolution created chaos in the Chinese government, from which it is still recovering today.

Liu Shao-chi was the first to fall from favor. Led by Lin Piao's troops, the cultural revolutionists established what amounted to martial law in Peking. Within a matter of months Vice Chairman Liu and his followers—fully half of the top leadership of the country—were disgraced and driven from power. Many were imprisoned. Others were shot.

It was during this period that Mao's wife, Jiang Qing, had her own first taste of authority. And it was during this period that she and her youthful Red Guard allies committed the ruthless excesses that after Mao's death were to lead to her trial and conviction for crimes against the government. Jiang Qing's official title was Vice Chairman for Cultural Affairs. Unofficially she became a kind of Lady High Executioner whose disfavor could mean disgrace and death.

Despite the chaos created by the Cultural Revolution, in 1970, on the twenty-first anniversary of the People's Republic of China, Mao was hailed by the masses of the Chinese people as their great savior. He was lavishly praised as having done more in twenty-one years for the country's economic development, public health, and education, the modernization of society, and the fostering of national patriotism than any other leader in the nation's history. At least some of this was true. Most of it Mao himself believed.

When Mao had first taken over the leadership in China he had insisted that he would never allow any cult of leadership to develop. No streets were to be named after Chinese Communist heroes. No towns or cities were to bear his or any of his colleagues' names. In the beginning Mao was quite sincere about this. But as his years in power passed and the Cult of Mao sprang up, he did little to stop it from developing and growing into a virtual religion. During the early stages of the Cultural Revolution Mao posters appeared in all the major towns and cities. And it was during this period that Mao's Little Red Book of *Quotations from Chairman Mao Tsetung* became a kind of national bible. Ironically, nothing so much proved that Mao was a human being as his acceptance of this attempt to deify him.

But Mao's godlike qualities were not accepted by all the Chinese people, and certainly not by all his comrades and colleagues. Among those who became disillusioned with the Chairman was Mao's old comrade of the Long March, now Defense Minister, Lin Piao.

Lin Piao opposed the Cult of Mao. He thought his old friend was losing sight of his own revolutionary beginnings when he seemed to bask in the hero worship rather than put an end to it. Lin also was sickened by the excesses of the Cultural Revolution and held Mao directly responsible for them. Lin also indicated that he too was human by wanting to take over Party leadership himself.

In 1971 Lin and his son, Lin-kuo, began a plot to overthrow Mao. They and a handful of fellow conspirators hatched a plan to assassinate Mao while he was touring in southern China. The plot was discovered—perhaps through a tip to Chou En-lai from Lin's daughter, Lin Li-heng—and the conspirators fled the country by airplane on September 13. Two hours later the plane crashed in Mongolia and Lin, his wife, and his son were killed. No explanation for the crash was ever given.

During the late 1960s and early 1970s Mao's leadership was also threatened by trouble right on the doorstep of the People's Republic of China. This was the Vietnam War, in which the United States was heavily engaged in supporting the South Vietnamese attempt to defeat Communist North Vietnam. Much like Korea, Vietnam had been divided after World War II and a war had developed to unify the country. Once again the United States had chosen to go to war against what its leaders saw as Communist aggression, this time on the part of the North Vietnamese. Actually the conflict was a civil war.

There were several members of the Chinese Politburo who

favored sending troops to the aid of North Vietnam's Vietcong forces, but Chairman Mao flatly opposed Chinese intervention. Because it was a civil war, he thought China should keep hands off. Nevertheless, early in the war he did allow several antiaircraft divisions from the People's Liberation Army to be sent to Hanoi to defend the North Vietnamese capital from bombing attacks by U.S. aircraft. These troops were withdrawn in 1968.

Mao was convinced that the Vietcong would win the war without Chinese intervention, but he did permit Vietcong troops to be trained in China and furnished North Vietnam with military supplies. He also made it clear that an American invasion of North Vietnam might well trigger Chinese intervention—just as it had in Korea.

Mao's prediction about a Vietcong victory proved correct when President Richard Nixon began pulling American troops out of Vietnam in the early 1970s. According to historian Ross Terrill, Mao later commented, "The United States can't be considered so powerful if it gives up after losing 50,000 men."

The Vietnam War would prove to be the only war that the United States had ever lost. As it neared its end there occurred a dramatic breakthrough in Chinese-American diplomatic relations.

Chou En-lai in northern Shaanxi shortly after the Long March. *US-China Peoples Friendship Association*

Mao delivers a speech to military students at a war college just before World War II. As soldiers these students later helped China defeat the Japanese. *US-China Peoples Friendship Association*

The special recognition given Generalissimo Chiang Kai-shek and Madame Chiang included inviting them to attend a high-level conference of Allied leaders at Cairo, Egypt, during World War II. Seated (left to right) are Chiang, U.S. President Franklin D. Roosevelt, British Prime Minister Winston Churchill, and Madame Chiang, the only female conferee. General Joseph Stilwell's rear-rank relationship with the Chiangs is indicated here by his position in the second row directly behind President Roosevelt (fifth from right). The British officer in the dark naval uniform is Admiral Louis Mountbatten, famed Combined Forces Commander in the China-Burma-India Theater. *U.S. Army Photo*

Chinese peasants on a commune during the early Mao regime prepare a field for planting. Such hand labor was identical to that done by Chinese peasants for centuries. *United Nations Photo*

Late in the Mao regime the woman manager of a state farm near Peking poses with the farm's tractor. Even today, however, much farm work is done without the aid of machinery. *Wide World Photo*

A young Chinese proudly holds aloft a Red Guard's banner at a pro-Mao Communist rally in Shanghai during the Cultural Revolution. *Wide World Photo*

Chairman Mao (left) with his Defense Minister, Lin Piao, at a 1966 rally in Peking. At this time Lin was regarded as Mao's closest aide and his probable successor. Later Lin was accused of leading a plot to assassinate Mao, but instead met death himself in an airplane crash that was never explained. *Wide World Photo*

Hua Guofeng is shown making his first public appearance as the successor to Mao Tsetung as Communist Party Chairman. Hua had made a deathbed promise to Mao that he would protect Mao's widow, Jiang Qing, but he later had her arrested and brought to trial as a member of the infamous Gang of Four. *Wide World Photo*

17

Ping-Pong Diplomacy
With the West

Ever the realist, Mao had begun to realize that the time was ripe for renewing Red China's relationship with the West. For one thing, he feared the Soviet Union's growing military strength and the threat that strength posed to China. He also realized that the unstable conditions caused by the Cultural Revolution had served to isolate his country from the rest of the world.

Mao decided that his first overture must be made toward the United States. And in 1971 an event occurred that enabled Mao to make the first move in his budding pro-Western foreign policy in an unusual way. The event was a Ping-Pong tournament.

Ping-Pong, or table tennis, had long been a popular sport in China. Mao himself was a devoted player, and Chinese teams usually dominated world table-tennis tournaments. In the spring of 1971 a top American Ping-Pong team visited Japan to take part in the World Table Tennis Championships. The Chinese team once again proved to be the undisputed leader in this meet. After it was over, several American players told their Chinese opponents they would like to visit China. A cable was dispatched to Peking, where Chou En-lai himself turned down the request. But Chairman Mao countermanded his top aide's order. As usual, Chou accepted Mao's decision with good grace, and within a matter of days the United States Ping-Pong players became the first Americans to make a semi-official visit to China since the 1950s.

China's new Open Door policy toward the West soon began to pay dramatic foreign policy dividends. President Nixon's National Security Adviser and later Secretary of State, Henry Kissinger, visited China twice during the next few months, and in February 1972 President Nixon himself flew to Peking for a week-long round of talks with Chairman Mao.

The meeting between Nixon and Mao was a delicate one. Nixon was an avowed and lifelong foe of Communism, and the United States was still fighting Communists in Vietnam. (The war did not officially end there until the following year.) Mao himself was noted for his outspoken and even violent anti-Americanism, and many of his colleagues strongly opposed their leader's apparent sudden shift in attitude. The biggest stumbling block of all, of course, was that there was no official relationship between the United States and the People's Republic of China. This situation was exactly what Mao wanted to change, and Nixon was apparently not averse to the idea.

"The week that changed the world," as the meeting was

heralded as, went off surprisingly well. Both Soviet and Western government officials were at first astonished by the fact that the dedicated Communist Mao and the dedicated anti-Communist Nixon had decided to get together at all. They were further taken aback by the warm expressions of friendship and plans for close future relations between the two leaders and their countries that seemed to grow out of the meeting.

Neither man would be in office to see the final results made possible by this initial breakthrough in the long and mutual misunderstanding between their two nations. Mao was to die before those results were achieved, and Nixon would be forced to resign the Presidency because of scandals within his administration. But during President Jimmy Carter's term in office the United States would officially recognize the People's Republic of China, on January 1, 1979.

During his last years Mao was stricken with Parkinsonism, a disease of the central nervous system. For a time he was physically unable to write and had to dictate all official correspondence as well as his own personal writing to an aide. A physical fitness buff almost to the end, however, Mao went for several lengthy and much-publicized swims in the Yangtze River to prove to his people that he was still physically capable of governing. Mentally, he remained alert and continued to move the People's Republic of China toward economic growth along strict socialist-state lines. He also tried to modify the excesses of the Cultural Revolution.

Chiang Kai-shek died on Taiwan on April 5, 1975, following a heart attack. He was eighty-seven. Mao made no public comment about his old rival's death. Chiang was succeeded as Premier of Nationalist China by his son, Chiang Ching-kuo.

Mao and the world were made even more aware of the

passing of China's old guard with the death of Chou En-lai the following year.

And Chairman Mao's personal Long March came to an end with his own death just a few months later.

On his deathbed the eighty-three-year-old Mao had called the entire Chinese Politburo to his side. One of the things he instructed them to do was to "Help Jiang Qing." Then he added several words that were not clearly intelligible. Some said the words were "to carry the Red Flag." Others insisted Mao said "to correct her errors."

When she was brought to trial for treason, Mao's widow insisted, of course, that Mao had passed on his authority to her by requesting the Politburo to "help Jiang Qing to carry the Red Flag." Her jurors chose to believe Mao had requested that they help his widow "correct her errors," and proceeded to do so by finding her guilty and sentencing her to death.

The men who came into power after Mao's death also tried to correct what they thought were Mao's own errors. When the People's Republic of China was first established, for a time there was great improvement in the nation's economy. Then once again the economy began to falter. One of the reasons for this stagnation was Mao and his people's refusal to be realistic about economic production. This was especially true in the case of agriculture.

Under each Five Year Plan the central planners in Peking would announce farm production goals for the nation. Then the Communist Party members in the provinces, towns, and villages would urge the peasants to meet these goals. The peasants would loyally strive to do so, but when they did not, this fact was not always reported to Peking. Not wanting to disappoint Chairman Mao and the central planners, the rural

Communist cadres would report that the goals had been met. This, of course, resulted in false production figures for the nation as a whole, a fact that was not realized until food shortages began to occur. Much the same situation held true in factories.

The post-Mao planners set about remedying this situation, but they have not always been successful. One of the basic flaws, as many economists have pointed out, is in the very nature of the socialist state and central planning itself. This the Communist leaders are not ready to admit, but it is nonetheless true and has been true in every Marxist-Leninist country from the Soviet Union on down.

For one thing, central planning to the strict degree that it was carried out in a strictly socialist state such as Red China under Chairman Mao ignores human nature and human self-interest. People simply will not work as hard to produce things for the state as they will to produce things for themselves. Under Chairman Mao, for example, agricultural land was divided among the peasants into huge farm cooperatives where all workers were to produce and share alike. Each farmer, however, was also given his own small plot of ground. Here the farm family could grow their own crops for their own use or to sell in the local market. Time and again it was shown that these tiny, privately owned and privately worked gardens outproduced the nearby agricultural cooperatives by as much as ten to one. Much the same results have consistently been shown in the Soviet Union.

Mao never really solved this problem, but the leaders who have come after him have tried to do so by introducing somewhat more capitalistic agricultural methods. Individual incentives, such as more pay for more production and greater recognition for individual achievement, have steadily been introduced into China since Mao's day. Most importantly, the government has adopted what is called the "responsibility system." Much of the country's farmland has been returned to individual farm families who are held responsible for peak production.

Central planning also falls down badly in the manufacturing area, a fact that Mao's successors have just begun to face. In industry the flaw in central planning results from a stubborn attempt by the government to distribute resources and decide what should be produced and how much rather than letting the demands of the marketplace influence these decisions. If the planners decide a factory should make steel nuts when all of the consumers want bolts, steel nuts are manufactured— and nobody buys them. Steel nuts soon are stockpiled in one place, and other factories that might be producing bolts are idle. Managers and workers soon have no incentive to maintain high production, and when extra effort does not result in increased earnings, the situation is made even worse. The whole industry is thrown out of balance.

In an effort to overhaul Red China's ailing economy, the government began to experiment with various capitalistic free-market practices in the early 1980s. A small but important example was the opening of a few privately owned and operated restaurants in several major cities. In the private sector, the Chinese government has stopped assigning all workers to specific jobs at fixed pay. Tax exemptions and low-interest loans have been offered to the self-employed. Some forty million Chinese enter the job market each year. Of these it has been estimated that more than two million will become self-employed or work for privately owned enterprises. In the industrial area, bonuses and higher wages began to be offered to foremen and factory workers who attained production goals. And not only were manufacturing plants allowed to make profits, but central planners began to demand that they do so.

In addition to introducing some of capitalism's personal incentive and free enterprise methods, the People's Republic of China has welcomed more and more foreign visitors. Tourism in China has increased more than tenfold since Mao's death and has brought in not only new ideas from the West but also welcome foreign money. In many ways, however, China continues to be a closed society, and tourists find they are only allowed to visit certain areas and take carefully chosen government-sponsored tours. Late in 1982 these restrictions were eased somewhat, and foreign travelers were allowed to visit some thirty additional cities in several previously restricted provinces. Some tourists were also allowed to visit China on an individual basis.

Relations between the People's Republic of China and the United States gradually improved after President Nixon's visit and official recognition of mainland China under President Carter. Trade between the two nations increased to about $7 billion a year, six times above the previous level. But relations began to deteriorate after Ronald Reagan became President in 1981. Taiwan has remained a sticking point between the Reagan administration and the administration in Peking.

Reagan, as outspoken a foe of Communism as Nixon, has balked at accepting mainland China as *the* China and rejecting the island of Taiwan's unrealistic claim to that title. Actually, Taiwan is what amounts to a separate province of China, but Reagan and others from the old China Lobby days continue to be reluctant to accept this reality. There have been strong indications that they want to continue the fiction that there are "two Chinas"; apparently they remain hopeful that Taiwan might one day regain the mainland.

Despite warnings from Peking, the Reagan administration has continued to sell weapons to the Nationalist Chinese government on Taiwan. To Peking this means that the United States does not want a strong and healthy relationship with Red China. To Reagan this means he "simply does not want to abandon an old friend." The Reagan administration, of course, wants to retain mainland China as a strong ally to act as a buffer between the United States and the Soviet Union, which Reagan regards as America and the Free World's number-one enemy.

On its part, China needs U.S. backing in its own continuing difficulties with Russia. To help its economy China also badly needs oil, and American oil companies want to negotiate South China Sea oil exploration rights. Whether Sino-American relations will improve or deteriorate depends partially on whether President Reagan's anti–Red China views moderate—as Nixon's did—and the United States recognizes China's sovereignty over Taiwan. It also depends somewhat on what position China's new leaders of the 1980s adopt in this controversy and others.

That there will soon be many new Chinese leaders there is little doubt. In September 1982 China's Communist Party adopted a new constitution to guide the country into the next century. The seventy-eight-year-old Deng Xiaoping retained his post as Vice Chairman, but there was a shake-up in the rest of the party hierarchy. Most importantly, the post of Party

Chairman that Mao Tsetung had created fifty years earlier was abolished.

But Mao was not forgotten. In announcing the adoption of the new constitution, Vice Chairman Deng spoke of the current campaign to revitalize China. This too, he pointed out, had been Chairman Mao's great goal. "And without Mao," he said, "there would be no People's Republic of China." Then Deng said that Mao had erred in letting himself become isolated from his great strength, the Chinese people. This had resulted, Deng said, in the mistakes of the Cultural Revolution. But Deng made it clear that he held Jiang Qing and others more responsible than Mao for these mistakes. Then he added: "Let us not forget that even tomorrow's Chinese government as well as the governments that will surely follow all will owe a great debt to Chairman Mao and the men, women, and children who once, long ago, made the Long March."

It was perhaps Chairman Mao's most fitting epitaph.

Further Reading

The classic book about the Long March and the one to which all readers and writers about the period are indebted is American journalist Edgar Snow's *Red Star Over China*. Snow entered the forbidden interior of China in 1936 and was the first Westerner to interview Mao Tsetung. He was also the first to tell the story of Mao's life, the Long March, and the Chinese revolution. *Red Star Over China* is highly readable, and its revised edition contains thumbnail biographies of Mao and his contemporaries. It is now published in paperback by Bantam Books, Inc., New York, 1978.

Snow wrote widely on China for several decades—he died in February 1972, the same week President Richard Nixon visited Peking—and recently his widow, Lois Wheeler Snow, compiled a collection of these writings under the title *Edgar Snow's China* (New York: Random House, Inc., 1981). This book is not only a splendid introduction to the work of the outstanding Western authority on Red China—Snow was trusted and revered by the Chinese Communist leaders—but also contains a truly outstanding collection of more than 450 pictures of the period.

British journalist Dick Wilson's *The Long March 1935* (New York: The Viking Press, Inc., 1971) is especially valuable for the lengthy quotations it contains from the accounts of Long March survivors. Other valuable survivors' accounts are in *Recalling the Long March,* by Liu Po-cheng and others, and *On the Long March as Guard to Chou Enlai,* by Wei Kuo-lu, both published by the Foreign Language Press, Peking, 1978. The Foreign Language Press has also published *The Selected Military Writings of Mao Tsetung* for more advanced readers. These three books are available in paperback from bookstores specializing in Asian publications. A copy of Mao's Little Red Book, *Quotations From Chairman Mao Tsetung,* can also be obtained from such bookstores. Locating such stores can be interesting as well as rewarding.

An excellent periodical is the *U.S.–China Review,* published bimonthly in Los Angeles by the U.S.–China Peoples Friendship Association. Its articles help keep readers, young and old, up-to-date on post-Mao developments in China.

Although much has been written on the Long March and the Chinese Revolution, not too many books are available on this period for younger readers. A good one is Robert Goldston's *The Long March* (New York: Franklin Watts, Inc., 1971).

Books for more mature readers are numerous. A few of the better recent ones are listed below:

Bonavia, David. *The Chinese*. New York: Lippincott & Crowell, 1980.

de Crespigny, R.R.C. *China, This Century*. New York: St. Martin's Press, Inc., 1975.

Fraser, John. *The Chinese: Portrait of a People*. New York: Summit Books, 1980.

Howard, Roger. *Mao Tsetung and the Chinese People*. New York, London: Monthly Review Press, London, 1977.

Morwood, William. *Duel for the Middle Kingdom*. New York: Everest House, 1980.

Peyrefitte, Alain. *The Chinese—Portrait of a People*. Indianapolis, New York: The Bobbs-Merrill Company, Inc., 1977.

Roberson, John R. *China—From Manchu to Mao*. New York: Atheneum Publishers, 1980.

Terrill, Ross. *Mao—A Biography*. New York: Harper & Row, Publishers, 1980.

Students interested in further reading about American General Joseph Stilwell's courageous and frustrating experiences in China during World War II should by all means read his own personal account. This is in *The Stilwell Papers,* edited by Theodore H. White, and published by William Sloane Associates, Inc., New York, 1948.

Far and away the best writing on the Stilwell period—as well as on several others—has been done by Barbara Tuchman. Her *Stilwell and the American Experience in China* (New York: The Macmillan Company, 1970, 1971) is must background reading for anyone hoping to understand U.S.–China relations today. There are also several essays—especially "If Mao Had Come to Washington"—in her more recent book, *Practicing History* (New York: Alfred A. Knopf, Inc., 1981), that shed much light on a dark period in the history of American diplomacy.

Index

Numbers in *italics* refer to illustrations.

96 97 99
1 1 - 1

NO RENEWALS!

**PLEASE RETURN BOOK AND REQUEST
AGAIN.**